ROUTLEDGE LIBRARY EDITIONS: LIBRARY AND INFORMATION SCIENCE

Volume 63

OPERATIONAL COSTS IN ACQUISITIONS

OPERATIONAL COSTS IN ACQUISITIONS

Edited by
JAMES R. COFFEY

LONDON AND NEW YORK

First published in 1991 by The Haworth Press, Inc.

This edition first published in 2020
by Routledge
2 Park Square, Milton Park, Abingdon, Oxon OX14 4RN

and by Routledge
52 Vanderbilt Avenue, New York, NY 10017

Routledge is an imprint of the Taylor & Francis Group, an informa business

© 1991 The Haworth Press, Inc.

All rights reserved. No part of this book may be reprinted or reproduced or utilised in any form or by any electronic, mechanical, or other means, now known or hereafter invented, including photocopying and recording, or in any information storage or retrieval system, without permission in writing from the publishers.

Trademark notice: Product or corporate names may be trademarks or registered trademarks, and are used only for identification and explanation without intent to infringe.

British Library Cataloguing in Publication Data
A catalogue record for this book is available from the British Library

ISBN: 978-0-367-34616-4 (Set)
ISBN: 978-0-429-34352-0 (Set) (ebk)
ISBN: 978-0-367-36200-3 (Volume 63) (hbk)
ISBN: 978-0-367-36205-8 (Volume 63) (pbk)
ISBN: 978-0-429-34457-2 (Volume 63) (ebk)

Publisher's Note
The publisher has gone to great lengths to ensure the quality of this reprint but points out that some imperfections in the original copies may be apparent.

Disclaimer
The publisher has made every effort to trace copyright holders and would welcome correspondence from those they have been unable to trace.

Operational Costs in Acquisitions

James R. Coffey
Editor

The Haworth Press
New York • London

Operational Costs in Acquisitions has also been published as *The Acquisitions Librarian*, Number 4 1990.

© 1991 by The Haworth Press, Inc. All rights reserved. No part of this work may be reproduced or utilized in any form or by any means, electronic or mechanical, including photocopying, microfilm and recording, or by any other information storage and retrieval system, without permission in writing from the publisher. Permission does not extend for any services providing photocopies for sale in any way. Printed in the United States of America.

The Haworth Press, Inc., 10 Alice Street, Binghamton, NY 13904-1580
EUROSPAN/Haworth, 3 Henrietta Street, London WC2E 8LU England

Library of Congress Cataloging-in-Publication Data

Operational costs in acquisitions / James R. Coffey, editor.
    p. cm.
    "Has also been published as The acquisitions librarian, number 4, 1990" – CIP t.p. verso.
    Includes bibliographical references.
    ISBN 1-56024-008-3 (acid free paper)
    1. Acquisitions (Libraries) – Costs. 2. Library finance. I. Coffey, James R.
Z689.063   1991   90-49254
                                                                                                                           CIP

Operational Costs in Acquisitions

CONTENTS

Introduction: Costing Acquisitions: Getting More for Less *James R. Coffey*	1
The Cost of Pre-Order Searching *Karen A. Schmidt*	5
Introduction	5
Pre-Order Searching: A Survey	7
Vendor Needs	15
Survey Conclusions	15
Cost Analyses	16
Pre-Order Searching Rationalized	18
Costs of Managing Exceptions to the Work Flow in Acquisitions Departments *Alicia M. Morris*	21
Introduction	21
Cost Factors	22
Benefits	28
Suggestions	29
Cost Impact on Acquisitions in Implementing an Integrated Online System *Doug Phelps*	33
Direct Costs	34
Labor Costs	35
Non-labor Costs	41
Conclusion	45

Costs of Automating Serials Acquisitions 47
Charles A. Le Guern

Vendor Selection 48
Implementation 49
Cost Analysis 49
Increased Ordering 50
Conclusion 53

Identifying Personnel Costs in Library Acquisitions 55
James R. Coffey

Introduction 55
Cost Overview 57
Interviewing and Hiring 59
Employee Attitudes 61
Training 62
Consultation 64
Performance Evaluation 65
Non-productive Time 66
Mistakes 67
Absenteeism 68
Staff Development 69
Measuring Service and Productivity 69
Conclusion 72

The Cost of Public Relations in Acquisitions 75
Katina Strauch
Bruce Strauch

Case 1 76
Case 2 78
Case 3 81
Conclusion 83

The Cost of Payment: Library Invoice Payment Operations 85
Marcia L. Anderson

Accounting Controls 86
Administrative Controls 87

Classification Levels and Staffing Considerations	88
Organization and Inefficiency	89
Transaction and Record Retention Costs	90
Communication	91
Controlling Costs	92
Procedural Review	92
Monitoring the Budget	93
Vendors	94
Automation	96
Conclusion	96

The Cost of Processing Invoices   99
Marsha S. Clark

Determining Costs	100
Verifying the Correctness of the Invoice	100
Processing for Payment	101
Maintaining Files	102
Unresolved Payments	103
Step-by-Step	103
Implications	105
Conclusion	106

Costing Acquisitions: An Annotated Bibliography   109
Theodora T. Haynes

Background	110
Theory	112
Methodology	114
Applications	115
Bibliographies	117

Introduction:
Costing Acquisitions:
Getting More for Less

James R. Coffey

I have always had an unquiet feeling that the costs of operating in the library technical services environment were higher than they ought to be. These costs were a phenomenon that seemed certainly to be there but not always tangible and apparent to the everyday librarian; somewhat like the folk-tale notion of a compelling reality visible only to the eyes of a pure virgin. The operational budget figures are not always available automatically to the acquisitions librarian. In fact, they are not always broken down by department, nor always kept by the library. The materials budget is usually easily available; but what we spend on invoicing, automation, personnel, supplies, and on otherwise managing the workflow seems invisible, even though the expenditure must be there. It is not so elusive once one takes the time to start capturing it on paper and it does become compelling once one realizes how it can get out of hand. If we had an intimate acquaintance with the cost of doing everything, we would perhaps make different decisions about how we spend our time. In the world of publishing, and especially of bookselling, people usually know the cost of each step in the workflow and can argue convincingly for or against changes in the process based on what they cost. Booksellers fear the power of files to increase their item costs; some librarians, on the other hand, embrace them, never reckoning their cost for a moment. Granted that there are differences in how libraries and commercial establishments will operate, it remains true that libraries pay the same prices to operate as booksellers and other less poverty-stricken businesses. Booksellers are always in a panic about how much things cost; li-

© 1991 by The Haworth Press, Inc. All rights reserved.

braries, it seems, are starting to be, or will have to start to be and this may turn out to be the challenge of the nineties.

For the last ten years at least libraries have been grappling with problems which concern money—how to make the most of what we get. While we have not always been in a crisis management situation, we have been on the go constantly, keeping up with demands, getting the work out and unable to worry too much about analyzing costs. Our efforts seem to have been focused on how to get the job done efficiently and we have assumed perhaps that efficiency has meant cost effectiveness. The money crisis has not gotten easier, however, and we are still challenged to get more of a return on the investment of resources. It seems as if librarians will meet this challenge as they have done in the past; coping with change is not new to us. We've always identified the needs and of course have had no trouble getting the information we need.

This issue of the *Acquisitions Librarian* represents a first step in looking more closely at the costs of running an acquisitions department. The papers that follow deal with various aspects of the internal costs of the library acquisitions department. Each takes a specific area or function and discusses its fiscal perspective. The intent is to get the reader to think about what is the cost of what we do, what happens to make costs expand, and how what sometimes appears to be efficiency can be superfluous and costly. Since it doesn't appear likely that librarians will accept readily the notion of reduced service, it becomes incumbent upon us to find a way to reduce our unit costs.

The people who have contributed the articles here represent a great deal of experience in library acquisitions. Some of the things they have in common are the ability to question the process and to look critically at how they are spending their operating budgets. In examining these costs—and they have not looked at everything—we found that they can be articulated and they can be controlled; not easily, but with the same kind of determination that makes "Technical Services Types" find a way to get the job done. In any event, it seems as if we will not get a choice. Everything seems to cost more these days and the allocation of resources seems to leave us with less.

Far from being definitive, these articles open the door to consideration of how we can examine the acquisitions process and spend our resources better, getting value for every cent. I hope the door doesn't close after this. There is more to do in this area and the insights we have to share can be helpful to the library community. Our ability to keep a careful watch on how the money is spent will reflect competence and credibility on our part which will be useful when budgets are allocated. We have made suggestions for further investigation and hope that someone will be stimulated to join in the effort. It should be clear that more fundamental and detailed studies are called for; not just reflection, but some practical data that will give librarians a chance to measure their effectiveness and improve their performance. I hope the reader will find much of value in this issue and, if provoked to move further along than these articles take us, to contact me. I would be pleased to coordinate any further research.

Jim Coffey
Rutgers University-Camden Library
Camden, New Jersey

The Cost of Pre-Order Searching

Karen A. Schmidt

SUMMARY. Some form of pre-order searching is performed in all libraries prior to sending an order to a vendor. Pre-order searching may include a search for duplication only, or may provide any number of pieces of bibliographic information. An informal survey of the pre-order searching practices of a few libraries reveals that some libraries perform pre-order searching tasks which do not enhance the purchasing information and which supply bibliographic information not used later in the processing flow. A simple formula for determining costs of pre-order searching and a practical method for analyzing the cost and effectiveness of pre-order searching are presented.

INTRODUCTION

Pre-order searching encompasses a number of library operations which include, but are not limited to, determining if the library already holds the title in question, assessing the availability of the piece, establishing the cost of each item, determining accurate authority records, and finding acceptable catalog copy. It would appear that practically every library has its own definition of which of these and other procedures embrace pre-order searching, based in part on the automated systems available to each library and the organizational arrangements which each has made.

The discussion of pre-order searching offered here presents the results of an informal survey of how various libraries interpret pre-order searching, offers a method for determining the costs of pre-order searching, and attempts to rationalize the process as it relates

---

Karen A. Schmidt is Acquisitions Librarian, University of Illinois at Urbana-Champaign, 1408 West Gregory Drive, Urbana, IL 61801.

© 1991 by The Haworth Press, Inc. All rights reserved.

to the acquisition of library materials. For the purposes of this discussion, acquisitions includes the ordering, claiming, and receipt processes which libraries engage in to purchase materials for the collection. It will be seen that much of what is called pre-order searching has little or no impact on the library's ability to purchase any given item, and can be costly to the library. Many tasks which are part of pre-order searching procedures may have an impact on other technical processes, such as cataloguing, but they likely do not enhance the acquisitions process itself. The more entailed the pre-order searching process, the more difficult it is to assess the cost to the library, both in real dollars and in user satisfaction in receiving a title more promptly. There have been a few studies done in this area over the past several years, of which the 1964 study by Lazorick and Minder is probably the best-known.[1] In this study of the Pennsylvania State University library system, the authors proposed the philosophy of "adequate information," suggesting that there is a difference between the . . . "amount of searching needed to identify adequately a publication to be purchased with the amount of searching needed for complete bibliographic information."[2] While the study did not look at personnel costs, but rather at bibliographic sources, it raised an important point about the rationale behind pre-order searching and the amount of effort which should be given it. A later study by Groot proposed a formula for determining actual costs of pre-order searching and overlayed this with a discussion of the optimal tools to be used.[3] In a thorough analysis of processing of archival material, Maher illustrated two methodologies for using cost analyses in processing, and proposed three ways of measuring processing efficiency, all of which have some bearing on determining the cost of pre-order searching.[4]

The various formulae discussed in these and other articles provide useful methods for analyzing the cost effectiveness of pre-order searching, but do not address some of the basic questions concerning pre-order searching, including why the searching is done and for whom, and the length of time which pre-order searching adds to the acquisitions process. These questions should be answered first before determining cost analysis of the process.

PRE-ORDER SEARCHING: A SURVEY

To understand what pre-order searching actually consists of, a form of qualitative research was used to collect data from various libraries on this procedure. In this study, twelve academic libraries of various sizes from all regions of the country were polled and asked to describe their own pre-order search process, why it is done, the number and level of staff needed for the task, the acquisition and duplication level, and the amount of time needed to place orders through the pre-order search process. In addition, six vendors were queried about the type of information needed to fill orders and the causes for the greatest number of returned material. This process, while clearly not exhaustive, permits the sketching of general trends within libraries for handling pre-order searching and illuminates the discussion of the content and intent of this particular set of procedures. It has the added advantage of allowing a free range of discussion which a survey does not permit, and gives a wider view than the case study.

As might be expected, every library polled undertakes some form of pre-order searching for virtually all titles which are firm-ordered. The exceptions include titles which are not in Roman script, and some area studies acquisitions. The amount of pre-order searching which is done can be broken into four categories, depending on both the intent and the content of the pre-order process. Level I pre-order searching includes simply searching for duplication. Level II includes searching for duplication and for availability. Levels III and IV have roughly the same content, but very different intentions. Both include searching for duplication, availability, and correct catalog entry, but Level III searching uses the information gained in the catalog entry search later in the catalog process, while Level IV searching appears to disregard this information in the catalog process. Level I libraries include two very large and one medium-size library, while Levels III and IV include a mixture of libraries of various sizes. Only one library falls into the Level II category, but this one library's procedures are useful for comparison purposes.

As Table I illustrates, staffing grows as the amount of searching grows. Two of the Level I libraries do no pre-order searching in the

TABLE I. LEVEL OF PRE-ORDER SEARCHING
AND STAFFING LEVELS

Level of Searching	No. of Libraries	Avg. No. Staff Assigned to POS	Range of No. of Staff Assigned to POS
Level I	3	.8	0 - 2.5 FTE
Level II	1	.5	.5 FTE
Level III	4	1.9	1.0 - 3.5 FTE
Level IV	4	3.9	2.5 - 5.0 FTE

acquisitions areas, while one library does all searching for duplication. It is important to note that in the two libraries where no searching is done in the acquisitions area, pre-order searching does occur, but is accomplished by the selectors. In both instances, it was confirmed that, for the vast majority of titles, selectors check only for duplication in the collection, a process which is enhanced by having an automated order file which is available to all staff. It was estimated that selectors check some 5% of all orders in some other source, such as on-line catalogs (e.g., OCLC) or in foreign bibliographies. Overall, selectors in these two libraries have enough bibliographic information about each title to order it. In the third library in Level I, there is not an automated order file, so that it is incumbent upon acquisitions staff to check titles on order and in process to avoid duplication. In every library, regardless of level designation, whatever pre-order searching is done is handled by library assistants, described in all instances as non-professional staff with more skills and responsiblities than library clerical staff.

Libraries were asked why they perform pre-order searching. In every instance, duplication was cited as the foremost reason for this work. While this is particularly true during times of constricted budgets, many libraries felt duplication was an anathema regardless of the financial situation. One librarian noted that every duplicate showed up a fault in the procedures and that each had to be examined in this light to see what might be improved. Overall, libraries reported that pre-order searching for duplicates uncovered some 30-40% potential duplicates, which certainly justifies the effort. The Level II library also searched for availability of titles, a task easily done in this particular situation because of the wide range of automated files available. Domestic titles which were deemed out of print could then be handled differently at the outset, and this library felt that searching for availability during the pre-order process cut down on the level of vendor correspondence later. In this library, if a title could not be readily identified as available, as is often the case with foreign publications, the order was sent to an appropriate vendor anyway, with the available bibliographic information. Table II displays the average number of titles searched among all the libraries, and the average number of duplicates received. It should be noted that as the amount of searching increases, the number of du-

TABLE II. LEVEL OF SEARCHING AND DUPLICATION RATE

Level of Searching	Avg. No. of Titles Ordered Per Year	Avg. No. of Duplicates Per Year
Level I	30,000	34
Level II	32,000	41
Level III	18,500	98
Level IV	26,100	162

plicates does not decrease, a phenomenon which will be discussed later.

Libraries listed as Level III and IV were concerned about more than duplication and availability. Both types wanted to ascertain the correct entries for the author and for any series which might be attached to the title. In addition, some of the libraries have automated acquisitions systems which require searching an on-line data base, such as OCLC, and downloading matching records into the acquisitions file. Regardless of the availability or requirements of any given automated system, libraries in Level III consistently reported that searching for name and/or series authorities was an important component in the cataloguing process, and one library reported that this work in effect established a minimal level cataloguing record which was available to the user. In these libraries, this searching was not lost at the end of the acquisitions process, but was carried over into the rest of the processing, thus expediting getting the book to the user. In two of these libraries, the staff who perform pre-order searching also perform pre-catalog searching, so there is a high level of consistency. In the other two libraries, there is a high level of communication between the acquisitions and cataloging staff, from which flows a good deal of mutual trust. In Level IV libraries, this type of searching seemed to be done for the sake of having a "clean" order record. In most instances, whatever authority work was performed by acquisitions staff was repeated by cataloguing personnel after the book was received. One librarian felt that it was important to have an order record which was as close as possible to the final catalogue record, even though this library's automated acquisitions file was not available for public use and not integrated with the on-line public catalog. It is important to point out that some of this authority searching was done to avoid duplication of titles with complex series or corporate entries. However, since the information gained in this process was essentially lost in the cataloging process, libraries handling pre-order searching in this way were considered to be Level IV libraries.

One further question concerning the reasons for pre-order searching asked how much information is generally included on the order requests which come to the pre-order searching area. If, for example, an order request came in which listed a title only, or some vague reference to a book one had heard of or read about, then a higher level of pre-order searching would be essential. In fact, all libraries queried reported that orders came into the acquisitions area (in the case of Levels I and II libraries) or the pre-order searching area with complete publication data. The instances in which a publisher or author, or some other important piece of information was missing, were negligible. The orders had come through some organizational equivalent of a bibliographer, often with brochures attached.

Libraries were questioned about how long the pre-order search process takes. As is shown in Table III, Level I and II libraries had an average turnaround time of four days, while Levels III and IV libraries averaged ten to twelve days. The Level I library which did not have an automated acquisitions file took about ten days to check for duplication. In the other two libraries, which have automated order files, this time dropped to one to three days. It is interesting to note that in Level III libraries which are required to download on-line catalog records into an automated acquisitions system, the time spent in pre-order searching is longer by five to ten days than in those libraries which are not automated, or not automated in this way. In these instances, the pre-order process is subverted by the requirements of an automated system, a situation which must be factored in when assessing the costs of pre-order searching. All but one library handled rush orders in one to three days. One library, in Level IV, took five days to process and send out a rush order, because of the level of searching required.

Since avoiding duplication was an important reason for engaging in pre-order searching, a comparison of the average number of staff engaged in pre-order searching and the average number of duplicates was made. As can be seen in Table IV, Level I libraries had an average of only one more duplicate than Level IV libraries, while Level III libraries surprisingly had the highest number. More searching did not decrease the number of duplicates, although it did increase the number of staff needed. Overall, the duplication rates in all libraries was well under one percent.

TABLE III. LENGTH OF TIME TO PLACE ORDERS

Level of Searching	Avg. Length of Time To Place Orders, All Libraries	Range in Length of Time to Place Orders
Level I	4.3 days	1 - 10 days
Level II	4.0 days	4 days
Level III	12.0 days	4 - 25 days
Level IV	10.0 days	6 - 21 days

TABLE IV. COMPARISON OF DUPLICATION AND PRE-ORDER SEARCHING STAFFING LEVELS

Level of Searching	Avg. No. of Dups. Per Year	Avg. No. of Staff Assigned to POS	Avg. No. of Dups. Per Staff
Level I	34	.8	42.5
Level II	41	.5	41.0
Level III	98	1.9	51.6
Level IV	162	3.9	41.5

VENDOR NEEDS

As noted earlier, six vendors were contacted to see which pieces of information are needed to fulfill an order. In each company, the first response was the need for the ISBN number, followed by author and title information. These three items are the minimum amount of information needed to fill an order accurately. In two cases, vendors actually kept their inventory by the ISBN, so that orders coming into the company without this number had to be searched before fulfillment could be made. One company estimated that some 35-40% of the orders coming into the company arrive without the ISBN, or with an incorrect ISBN, delaying fulfillment by one to five days. Vendors expressed overall satisfaction with the information given by libraries, and gave concurring estimates that, over and above the ISBN problem, some 5-10% of all orders received had to be researched further for publisher or edition information. Rigid pricing parameters caused vendors problems, particularly when a library gave an estimated price based on some book cost average. This frequently causes unacceptable discrepancies which necessitate contacting the library before sending the book. While some libraries expressed concern that they not send orders for titles not yet published, none of the vendors considered that a problem area. One vendor noted that publishers are now advertising many titles well in advance of publication to ascertain the interest level from bookstores and libraries, and all vendors were equipped to keep NYP orders on their outstanding order files until the titles were available.

SURVEY CONCLUSIONS

The results of this mini-survey lead to several conclusions about the nature of pre-order searching:

— pre-order searching is done to avoid duplication;
— pre-order searching may also be done to provide additional bibliographic information, much of which seems unnecessary to the acquisitions process — any searching uncovering more than duplication and providing less than the ISBN and author/

title/publisher is not essential to having an order filled by a vendor;
— pre-order searching is most usually done on order requests which already have enough information to order the material;
— searching is handled by paraprofessional staff;
— automated order files speed the process of searching for duplication; automated acquisitions systems which read from and feed into on-line catalogs systems are likely to slow down the acquisitions process.

Perhaps the most troubling finding of all is the existence of library organizations in which pre-order searching appears to be taking place without rationalization or meaning. It is one thing to search and add bibliographic information to order records and to have that information used by another department for processing, once the order is received. It is quite another to search for bibliographic information for the sake of clean records or because of the demands of an automated system, and to have that information ignored once the book is in hand.

COST ANALYSES

It is relatively easy to see the financial implications of these three levels of pre-order searching, using the formula suggested by Groot for determining verification costs.[5] The formula she proposes states the following:

Cost = (no. of items) × (minutes/item) × (labor cost/minute)

Suppose a library needs to search 20,000 titles each year. This library has one paraprofessional earning $16,000 per year to handle the searching. The library in question has an automated order file integrated with an on-line catalog with automated authority files supporting it, i.e., a search on one terminal will reveal all records of items ordered or received or cataloged. Testing the amount of time it takes to search the order file and the on-line catalog reveals that, taking into account down time and slowed response times for the automation systems throughout the year, it takes one minute to perform and record the results of one search in the order file/on-line catalog. The library also is a contributing member of the OCLC data base, and if the searcher wishes to check for cataloging copy and record it or print it, it will take 1 1/2 minutes for every OCLC search. For the sake of accuracy in searching, it is assumed that the searcher will make two checks in the automated order file/on-line catalog, one for author-title and one for series.

If the library searches for duplicates only, the formula for figuring labor costs for one year is:

(items per year) × (2 min. per order file/on-line catalog search) × (labor cost/min.)

OR

20,000 × 2 × $.13 = $5,200/year

If the library searches for duplicates and also checks for cataloging copy, the formula becomes:

(items per year) × (2 min. per order file/on-line catalog search + 1.5 min./OCLC search) × (labor cost/min.)

OR

20,000 × (2 + 1.5) × $.13 = $9,100/year

Therefore, searching for cataloging copy as well as for duplicates costs 75% more for each title. This cost can be justified if the cataloging and bibliographic information which is found during the OCLC search is used for cataloging once the book is received. If, however, this information is not used, the costs can easily be doubled.

There are many reasons why the cataloging information found during the order process may not be used during the cataloging process, including the existence of better cataloging copy (e.g., DLC copy is available where before only member copy was available), updates in authority records which substantially change entries, or receipt and acceptance or a different edition or format. Unfortunately, not all reasons for ignoring bibliographic information provided through the pre-order search process are as noble. A lack of communication or trust between the two technical processing areas often interferes with the objective of efficiently and inexpensively getting material to the user and deteriorates into a plethora of duplicative procedures which only serve to hinder productivity.

PRE-ORDER SEARCHING RATIONALIZED

The cost analysis given above is simplistic and only intended to be illustrative of how measurements of the effectiveness of various forms of pre-order searching might be measured. As any one who has worked with pre-order searching will attest, all orders are not created equally, and each batch of orders, as it presents itself for pre-order searching, will contain a few titles which are difficult to handle. In addition, there are other costs which have not been factored in, including the cost of returning any duplicate requests to the requestor with salient information, and the costs of any number of minute record-keeping details, such as stamping, sorting and recording of statistics. Every library will present a different scenario, but one over-riding idea is clear: pre-order searching should include only those procedures which collect information of use to the vendor and which will avoid unnecessary duplication of titles in the library. Collecting and recording other information is useful if, and only if, this information is going to be used during the post-receipt process. Any other procedures are superfluous, costly to the library in terms of labor, and detract from the aim of getting the material to the user quickly.

There are ways of calculating the exact costs of pre-order searching without involving staff in minute recordkeeping for a long period of time. The easiest method is to take "snapshots" of the operation during a relatively short period of time. The first step is to list the exact sequence of the pre-order search process, being reasonably specific without becoming picayune. For example, a pre-order search routine might include the following:

— arranging and distributing the orders
— searching the order file and noting the findings
— searching for standing order duplication and noting the findings

— finding and recording the ISBN
— performing unique searches on difficult orders

Once the routine is broken into discrete steps, staff handling these activities can measure how many items can be handled during a short period of time (e.g., fifteen minutes). Repeating this "snapshot" several times over a two to four week period will provide an accurate record of the amount of time needed to perform each task. Using the annual salary of the staff handling the task broken down into cost per minute, one can easily figure the cost of each task using Groot's formula. Each task should then be analyzed to see if the cost justifies the expense. For example, if during the pre-order searching it is discovered that every author is searched for a name authority, it is essential to ask why. Does it clear up any misunderstanding a vendor may have in filling the order? Is it a requirement of the automated system being used in the library? It is useful to chart the routines of the post-receipt/cataloging processes to see if any overlap occurs in these tasks, and if the overlap is necessary. Certainly, there are occasions when overlap is inevitable, as in the case of searching series for potential duplication through standing orders. Religiously recording the LC entry for a series may not be essential, however, if this area is simply re-searched during the cataloging process.

All too frequently, procedures take on a life of their own. Libraries become wedded to routines through time, and the rationale for the procedures become blurred. Pre-order searching frequently is one of these procedures, and it is incumbent upon us to analyze constantly what and why we are handling our orders in any given way and how much it is costing in time and labor. If pre-order searching is in actuality pre-catalog searching, perhaps it should be renamed to reflect the assignment.

REFERENCES

1. Gerald J. Lazorick and Thomas L. Minder, "A Least Cost Searching Sequence," *College & Research Libraries* 25: 126-128 (March 1964).
2. Ibid., p. 126.
3. Elizabeth H. Groot, "A Comparison of Library Tools for Monograph Veri-

fication," *Library Resources & Technical Services* 25: 149-161 (April/June 1981).

4. William J. Maher, "Measurement and Analysis of Processing Costs in Academic Archives," *College & Research Libraries* 43: 59-67 (January 1982).

5. Groot, p. 152.

Costs of Managing Exceptions to the Work Flow in Acquisitions Departments

Alicia M. Morris

INTRODUCTION

The costs of acquiring and processing library materials have long been a concern of library professionals because of the continuing pressures of rising book prices, soaring personnel costs, the increasing costs of automation, and the net shrinking of operating budgets. Librarians have been required to look closely at costs involved in material acquisitions and have been forced to make some difficult decisions. The cancellation of subscriptions and the decision to cease collecting in certain subject areas because of the prohibitive costs of maintaining the collections are but two examples of how librarians have been forced to cope with inadequate materials budgets.

In an effort to control processing costs, technical services departments have been reorganized and functions have been combined to streamline material processing. Automation has allowed for the combination and redistribution of many processing functions resulting in an increase in productivity with little or no increase in staff size. In some acquisitions departments searching and ordering have been combined to eliminate the double handling of order requests. Personnel in copy cataloging departments are performing some of the work that was once the responsibility of original cataloging. This change also eliminates the double and triple handling of a cer-

---

Alicia M. Morris is affiliated with the University of Pennsylvania, Van Pelt Library, Philadelphia, PA 19104.

© 1991 by The Haworth Press, Inc. All rights reserved.

tain class of materials and frees original cataloging departments to catalog materials that previously would have gone directly into the technical processing backlog. One of the added benefits of these kinds of changes is that the type of work done by technical processing personnel has become more varied, and hopefully, more interesting.

While there has been discussion in the literature concerning technical services processing costs, much of what was found is dated, and there has been little attention given to understanding the costs of handling exceptions to the work flow (i.e., problems). This is a processing concern that if not treated systematically can result in costly and time consuming efforts on the part of technical services personnel. But it is also an area that seems to defy systematic methods of treatment. Exceptions by their very nature require individual attention, and problem resolution calls for the application of any number of procedures, some of which will have been defined if the problem was previously addressed, and others which will require the formulation of new procedures as unique situations are encountered. Everything depends upon where in the process the problem occurs.

This discussion will consider the factors involved in determining the costs of dealing with exceptions to the work flow, the benefits derived to the process of acquiring materials when exceptions encountered are addressed efficiently, and suggestions for reducing costs. The focus will center on the acquisition of currently published monographic materials. Firm orders will be the primary consideration, although many of the same costs apply to materials acquired as gifts or through library approval or blanket plans. The acquisition of serials and standing orders is beyond the purview of this discussion except as they relate to the problems encountered in the acquisition of monographs.

COST FACTORS

Exceptions to the work flow occur within the framework of the overall acquisitions process. Figure 1 describes in the form of a chart the basic steps involved in the acquisition of materials from the time a book is requested to the time it leaves the department for

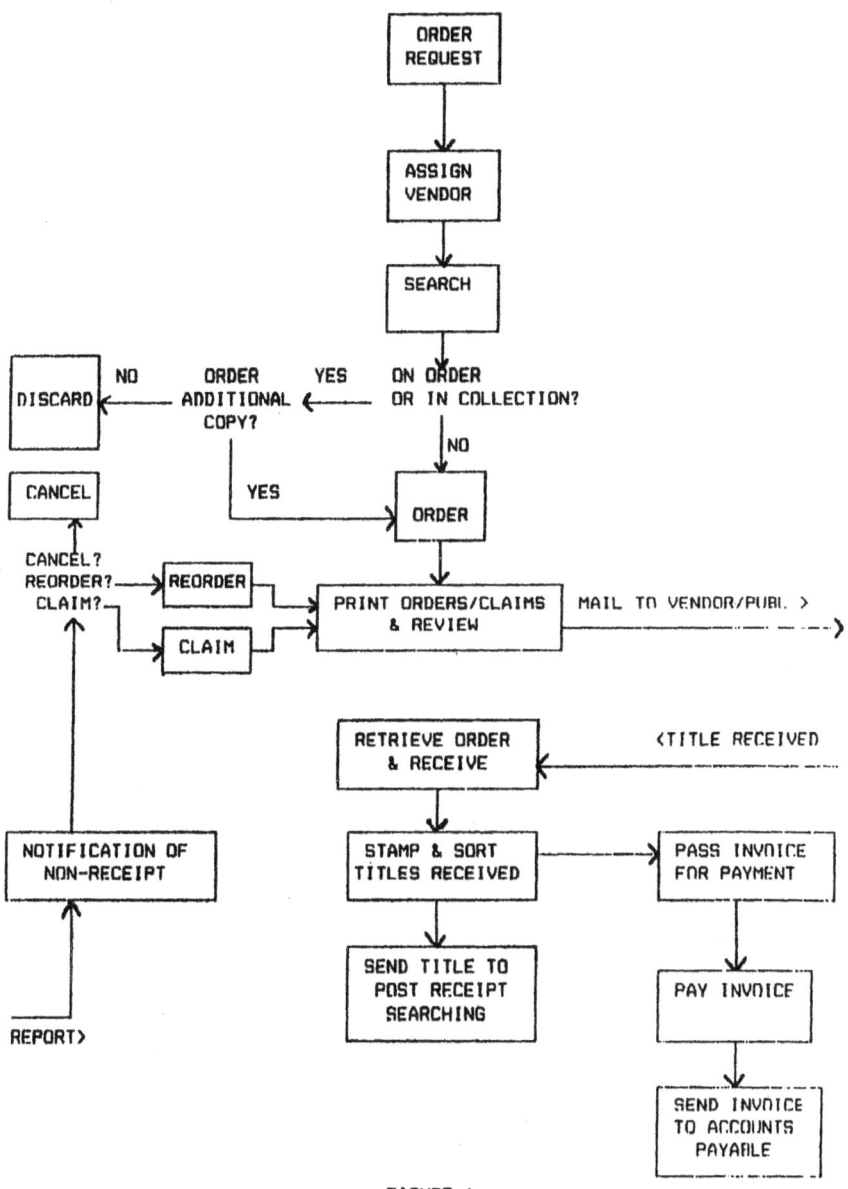

FIGURE 1

post receipt searching and cataloging. The actual processes involved are more complicated than the chart describes, but materials generally flow through the system in logical step-by-step procedures. Problems occur when exceptions to the established routines arise. In general, resolving a problem and placing the order request (or title received if the problem arises at the receipt stage) back into the normal processing routine require:

a. Identifying the problem
b. Backtracking to the source (often the original order)
c. Following the process through to the point where the problem occurred
d. Deciding on a solution
e. Informing (via phone, letter or computer) the necessary people of the problem and the action to be taken
f. Taking steps to correct the situation
g. Placing the order back into the normal processing routine

Exceptions can range from the routine to the complex. Handling exceptions can be as simple as cancelling a title on order that is later received as a gift or as complicated as figuring out who at your institution ordered twenty copies of a title that were shipped to the library, or tracking down two copies of a title that were delivered and signed for, but were never received in the acquisitions department. Costs incurred in handling exceptions to the work flow include database, telephone and postage charges, and charges for non-returnable items. However, the overwhelming costs of handling these exceptions are personnel costs. Typically, the most experienced and highest ranking members of the acquisitions department have the responsibility of resolving problems that fall outside the normal processing routines. A particularly difficult problem can consume the time of two or even three employees. There may be only two people whose responsibility it is to resolve problems out of a staff of ten, but because these two are typically the most senior employees (a librarian and a staff member) resolving problems can turn out to be an expensive operation when compared to the overall processing costs of the department.

It is easy to overlook this area of acquisitions processing when librarians initiate or renew efforts to contain costs and streamline processing functions because personnel costs are not generally considered in the cost of acquiring materials, and the responsibility of handling exceptions normally lies outside normal work flow routines.

There are several reasons why an examination should be made of how exceptions to the work flow are dealt with in an acquisitions department. The most obvious is to determine the cost to the department in terms of time spent in resolving problems as they arise. Another is to be able to compare these costs to the benefits derived to the overall functioning of the department. A third reason is that an understanding of exactly what kinds of exceptions or problems are encountered in the acquisition of materials enables technical services personnel to categorize and quantify these problems, and thus affords the possibility of grouping classes of exceptions that can be dealt with in similar ways. Normal procedures can be created for items that for one reason or another fall outside standard processing routines.

There are already some procedures that have commonly been established for work flow exceptions. Returning duplicates or items ordered in error to a library's major vendors is one example. If problems occurring with some amount of frequency can be classified and general procedures established to deal with them, then time spent addressing those problems can be reduced and a corresponding savings can be realized.

Tracking problems can also help in defining critical points in the process for identifying and resolving problems or errors. There is a point beyond which the time required to solve a problem rises dramatically. The following example illustrates this point.

> A dunning notice is received for non-payment of an invoice. The bookkeeper can find no record of payment and asks a member of the acquisitions staff to look into it. The pending file is checked and the unpaid invoice is found. One item on the invoice is not marked received. There is information contained on the invoice stating that the title in question is to be shipped separately. When the order is checked it is found that the title was received on a different invoice. That invoice is

checked and verified that the title was paid for. The staff member then searches the order file to verify that a second order was not placed for the title. No order is found. Since serial and monographic orders are sometimes charged on the same invoice (and the title in question contains a series statement), the serials department is consulted to make sure that there is no standing order for the title. There is no standing order for the title and it is concluded that the library was charged twice for the same item. The cost of the title received is deducted from the unpaid invoice and a letter is sent along with payment of the balance explaining the deduction.

The duplicate charge would have been caught upon receipt of the item if a note explaining the invoice problem had been placed on the order when the partial shipment was originally received. The bookkeeper would not have been involved and there would have been no need to search the invoice files to verify payment. In this example receipt of the title is the point at which the opportunity exists to limit the time required to solve the problem. Beyond the receipt stage other points in the process must be checked to verify payment status; and the people responsible for controlling those processes need to be consulted.

Exceptions that arise tend to correspond to the three major functions of an acquisitions department: the order, receipt and accounting functions. Problems occurring at the order stage tend to be easier to remedy than those occurring farther along in the acquisitions process because there are fewer points at which exceptions to the normal routine can occur. Exceptions to the receipt and accounting procedures become increasingly more complicated as the steps of identifying and resolving the problems become more involved. For example, when a book arrives whose title differs from the title ordered it must first be determined that what was received was in fact the title the library originally requested. It must then be ascertained that the correct title is not already on order or due to come in on a standing, approval or blanket order. If the correct title is on order or due to arrive automatically, the order must either be cancelled or the item in hand returned. If the item received is not the title originally requested it must be decided whether or not to keep the title received. This decision involves the department head or collection development personnel. If the title is kept the vendor must be notified that the incorrect title was received, that the library intends to keep it, and that the original order is still outstanding. The action taken must then be logged on the order to assist in answering future questions that may arise concerning the item.

The difficulty in trying to categorize exceptions to the work flow is in the many variations that can occur with any particular problem. The previous illustration is an example of the many decisions that must be made when dealing with an exception to the work flow. There are, however, broad categories that can be created to identify problems. For each of the processing functions they include the following:

A. Order

    1. Title identification
    2. Searching
    3. Price
    4. Ordering
    5. Claiming

B. Receipt

    1. Duplicate
    2. Order error
    3. Title identification
    4. Shipment error

C. Accounting

    1. Billing error
    2. Receipt error
    3. Returns
    4. Payment
    5. Budget reconciliation

If the kinds of problems that tend to occur in an acquisitions department can be identified, the steps required to resolve them can be logged and general procedures defined to deal with the problems.

Documenting procedures has several advantages. First and foremost, procedures identify the types of problems that occur frequently and provide instructions for their resolution. Procedures represent solutions to problems as they are handled in the department, and serve as vehicles for training personnel. Documented procedures also provide a basis for streamlining processes and expanding the collective experience of the department. As new problems arise solutions can be added to the existing documentation. Documentation also serves as a vehicle by which acquisitions personnel can become aware of the processing concerns of the department. If people are aware of the problems that occur they can take steps in their own work to reduce the frequency of occurrence. The end result is an overall savings to the department in time spent on dealing with problems.

BENEFITS

Identifying, categorizing and documenting exceptions enables librarians to examine the points at which problems tend to appear. Patterns or work flow bottlenecks that can be statistically measured can be used as justifications for instituting new methods to improve departmental efficiency. If orders requiring prepayments are found to take considerably longer to acquire than billable orders, creating deposit accounts with a publisher or placing orders with vendors who are willing to prepay for the library may be a more efficient way to acquire materials. Approval plans or publisher-based standing orders may be the solution for departments that are chronically understaffed and cannot maintain an acceptable turn around time in acquiring and processing material. Documentation of exceptions occurring due to publisher or vendor error can be used to provide input to vendor analysis. A library that has several shipping addresses requires that a supplier be flexible enough to handle variations in order instructions. This is particularly important for large libraries and libraries with branches dispersed over large areas. Identifying patterns in work flow exceptions can also serve as a gauge in assessing how well staff members perform their jobs. The occurrence of exceptions to the work flow will increase if people aren't trained properly. For example, an increase in the number of duplicates received for titles arriving on standing order can indicate that personnel in searching and ordering sections are insufficiently trained in identifying sets and series and the various ways these kinds of materials are acquired by the library. Once the problem is identified training procedures can be redefined to improve the quality of work produced and reduce the rate at which exceptions occur.

Classifying and documenting exceptions to the work flow also provides librarians with a vehicle with which quantifiable measurement can be made of the kinds of problems occurring in the acquisitions process. A clear understanding of the kinds of exceptions that occur can alert librarians to deficiencies in normal material processing work flow that can be remedied with procedural changes. It is also possible to routinize some exceptions, thus decreasing the amount of time spent correcting problems. Compiling statistics on work flow exceptions and the time spent resolving them provides an idea of the range of complexities of problems dealt with in an acquisitions department. It also provides a basis for decision making for resource allocation.

A final benefit that the process of handling exceptions to the work flow adds to the entire process of material acquisitions is quality control. The value of ensuring efficient and accurate acquisition and payment methods should not be underestimated. It is the ultimate criteria by which the quality of acquisitions operations is measured.

SUGGESTIONS

Given the fact that exceptions to the work flow are an inevitable occurrence in the day to day operation of acquisitions departments, the concern of the librarian must be to manage efficiently problems that fall outside the normal processing routine. A close study of the factors that cause exceptions to occur, a measurement of the frequency and the time taken to resolve problems will provide an idea of cost relative to the cost of all acquisitions processing. Armed with the knowledge of what happens, how often a problem occurs and how long it takes to resolve, steps can be taken to streamline the process and reduce costs.

Understanding the factors involved will illuminate training and communication problems regarding staff performance. Incomplete or outdated procedures can also be identified by examining the process leading to the problem. Documenting the frequency of occurrence and the time involved in resolving a particular problem provides a measure by which exceptions can be categorized from the simple to the complex. Problems occurring with some amount of frequency, and those of a relatively simple nature should be documented and procedures for handling them should be created. An improved understanding on the part of all acquisitions staff of the causes of exceptions to the work flow can alert personnel to the steps they can take to prevent problems from happening. For example, if everyone in the department is aware that the library receives university press titles on approval, then those in the searching section will know to question requests for titles published by a university press that contain no information acknowledging the fact that the title will also be coming on approval. The same holds true for the person placing the order. A mistake caught in the early stages of searching and ordering is a problem avoided. Making an effort to reduce the number of exceptions, and streamlining procedures where possible are two preventive measures to be taken to reduce the overall costs of dealing with exceptions to the work flow.

There are, however, exceptions that defy categorization by virtue of their complexity or infrequency of occurrence. Procedures for dealing with these kinds of exceptions will probably never be made part of a routine. Problems that cannot be anticipated will also fall within this category. An examination of the entire process will identify to what extent these more difficult problems occupy staff time. An evaluation of the benefit derived versus the time spent on resolving the more difficult problems that occur in the process will provide information for deciding the point at which it becomes necessary to terminate the entire effort, or begin anew the process of acquiring the item. The decision of course depends on how important it may be for the library to acquire the title. If the item is needed at any cost, then it may be necessary to perform an exhaustive search for it. Any amount of time spent by the library staff trying to locate the item is justifiable if a particular document is crucial to the research needs of the user. It is important to base decisions from a point of knowledge of how difficult it may be to acquire a title combined with an understanding of how important it is to obtain an item for the collection.

The cost of managing exceptions in the acquisitions work flow are identified by categorizing problems, documenting procedures, and measuring the time involved in resolving problems. Reducing costs entails creating processing routines for those exceptions that occur frequently or are relatively simple to solve, and instituting new methods to eliminate chronic problems in the acquisitions work flow. For infrequent and complex problems it is necessary to weigh the cost of ultimately acquiring the item with the benefit derived of having the title in the collection.

NOTES

Lisa J. Aren, Susan J. Webreck, and Mark Patrick, "Costing Library Operations—A Bibliography," *Collection Building* 8 (3), 1987, 23-28.

Constance Brutcher, Glen Gessford, and Emmet Rixford, "Cost Accounting for the Library," *Library Resources & Technical Services* 8 (4), Fall 1964, 413-431.

Malcolm Getz and Doug Phelps, "Labor Costs in the Technical Operation of Three Research Libraries," *The Journal of Academic Librarianship* 10 (4), 1984, 209-219.

Hershey, Johanna, "The Impact of the Implementation of NOTIS on the Technical Services Workflow at the Milton S. Eisenhower Library, Johns Hopkins University," *Cataloging & Classification Quarterly* 9 (1), 1988, 19-26.

Mandel, Carol A., "Trade-offs: Quantifying Quality in Library Technical Services," *Journal of Academic Librarianship* 14 (4), 1988, 214-220.

MacQuarrie, Catherine M., "Cost Survey: Cost of Ordering, Cataloging, and Preparations in Southern California Libraries," *Library Resources & Technical Services* 6 (4), Fall 1962, 337-350.

Betty Jo Mitchell, Norman E. Tanis, and Jack Jaffee, *Cost Analysis of Library Functions: A Total System Approach* (Greenwich, Conn.: JAI Press, 1978).

Piercy, Esther J. "Costs, Time, and Terms," *Library Resources & Technical Services* 6 (4), Fall 1962, 336.

Welch, Helen M. "Technical Service Costs, Statistics, and Standards," *Library Resources & Technical Services* 11 (4), Fall 1967, 436-442.

Cost Impact on Acquisitions in Implementing an Integrated Online System

Doug Phelps

SUMMARY. One of the problems in attempting to analyze the financial impact on technical processing of an integrated online system is the fact that the system both saves and adds costs. Though acquisitions had been automated since 1965, in mid-1986 the General Technical Services Division of the Vanderbilt University library finalized its migration to the acquisitions module of the integrated online system (NOTIS). Analysis of costs the following year (1987/88) showed a 38% increase for acquisition functions over a five year period. Costs associated with ordering indicated the most dramatic increases (61%) with those pertaining to receiving being close behind (59%). Correspondingly, production per hour worked was 47% lower in ordering for 1987/88 as compared to 1983/84 and 18% lower in receiving for the same period.

For two decades, the library serving Vanderbilt University has followed a budget theory of charging the constituent libraries for centralized technical services. First, as the Joint University Libraries, centralization of processing began with the Acquisitions Department in 1969. Other aspects followed during the next five years. By 1979, when Vanderbilt University absorbed George Peabody College and the joint ownership of library services melded into the single ownership by Vanderbilt, the pattern of charging for processing services was firmly established. During the past five years, the current library administration has refined the basis for charge assessments, placing more emphasis on cost analysis to de-

---

Doug Phelps is Director of General Technical Services, Vanderbilt University Library, 419–21st Avenue South, Nashville, TN 37240-0007.

© 1991 by The Haworth Press, Inc. All rights reserved.

termine the assessment figures more accurately. As a result, patterns of organization and workflow have shifted—and continue to shift—as the management of the General Technical Services Division attempts to refine and reduce the "bottom line" costs while maintaining (if not improving) the services offered.[1]

Because the cost analysis of technical services is budget-driven, attention is focused on the larger picture rather than on individual tasks within a particular function. Concern is more for analyzing the cost of acquisitions[2] rather than identifying how much it costs to order a RUSH title directly from the publisher instead of from a vendor. While acquisitions at Vanderbilt has been automated since 1965, the five years of cost data cover the merger of acquisition functions into a newly installed integrated online system.[3] While the data presented is specific to the Vanderbilt environment, some experiences and observations may be of assistance to librarians in other environments.

DIRECT COSTS

The most significant financial impact of the integrated online system was its initial cost. Implementation of the system, including the initial purchase of hardware was financed by the university and, therefore, did not figure into any acquisitions costs. Maintenance and other on-going costs were left to the library's budget.

The advent of the integrated online system necessitated the creation of a Systems Office within the library's administrative structure. Initially funded at one person (Assistant Director for Systems), by 1987/88 the office had grown to six full-time personnel plus programming support from the University Computer Center. The cost of this growth is included as part of the on-going cost of the automated system.

The budget theory of Vanderbilt University calls for distributing the library's system costs among the various operating divisions of the library. The initial paradigm divided the total annual cost by the number of terminals having access to the system, thus deriving a cost per terminal. As a result, the automated system assessment to the acquisition-related functions jumped from zero in 1983/84 to $7,873 in 1985/86. In mid-1986, General Technical Services activated the acquisitions module of the integrated online system and assigned terminals to the order/receive staff of Acquisitions. By 1987/88 the assessment to acquisition-related units had increased to $17,291, as shown in Table 1. Re-interpreted as cost per volume received in Acquisitions, the data shows an assessment of $0.57 per volume in 1987/88.

From the first year of the assessment to the most recent year completed, a period of three years, the automated system cost assessed to acquisition functions increased 120%. During the years covered by this particular study, a period of only five years, the direct cost to acquisition functions went from zero to $17,291.

The automated system assessment and the portion of the library administration assessment which is attributable to the Systems Office measure only the direct cost and do not take into consideration the question of impact on acquisition operations by the integrated online system. To measure this impact — at least from a cost perspective — one compares the various elements of the acquisition functions during this five year period.

LABOR COSTS

One of the problems in attempting to analyze whether an integrated system saves or adds cost to technical processing is the fact that it does both. An automated system permits routine activities to be done differently. For the most part, the more clerical the activity the more effective the impact of automation. At the same time, an integrated system may require new routines. This is especially true in acquisitions. Records are no longer "just" acquisitions records. They belong to the system and therefore require a different approach to recording data so that the system as a whole can benefit. It is possible to measure staff activity and the costs involved before and after implementing an integrated online system and to compare these measurements.

To determine labor costs, one must first identify the factors involved. Precisely what activity or activities constitute acquisitions? What is the production unit for this activity (i.e., volumes, titles, orders placed, claims issued, etc.)? Who participates in these activities? What is the average labor cost per hour?[4] For how many hours

TABLE 1: AUTOMATED SYSTEM ASSESSMENTS TO ACQUISITIONS-RELATED ACTIVITIES 1983/84 AND 1987/88.

	1983/84	1987/88
VOLUMES RECEIVED	36,071	29,932

	1983/84			1987/88		
	No. of Terminals	Assessment	Cost per Volume	No. of Terminals	Assessment	Cost per Volume
Verification	0	$0	$0	4	$8,645	$0.29
Data Entry	0	0	0	0	0	0.00
Ordering	0	0	0	2	4,323	0.14
Receiving	0	0	0	2	4,323	0.14
Invoice Payment	0	0	0	0	0	0.00
	0	**$0**	**$0**	**8**	**$17,291**	**$0.57**

of the activity has the library paid each person? The average labor cost per hour multiplied by the total hours paid yields the labor cost of the activity.

Table 2 shows the distribution of hours for the years under comparison. The hours shown represent hours for which the library made payment; therefore they include vacation, sick leave, break time, meetings, etc.

The distribution of labor for acquisition-related activities dropped 25% between 1983/84 and 1987/88. Obviously, without a controlled environment, one cannot attribute the change solely to the integrated online system. On the other hand, one cannot dismiss the impact of such a radical alteration of the environment.

Since the number of paid hours can reflect many extraneous factors, including position vacancies due to staff turn-over, a more appropriate comparison is the number of units produced for each hour *worked*. Although "hours worked" are a secondary part of the formula in this particular approach to cost analysis (since "cost" must also include payment for time not worked, such as vacation and sick leave), the measure of production per hour worked gives an interesting comparison of before and after implementation of the integrated acquisitions module. Table 3 presents this data.

The production units for which there is sufficient data for comparison show a 6% increase, in the aggregate, for units produced per hour. However, the order/receive functions show a 47% decrease and an 18% decrease respectively. Were one to consider only these core acquisitions activities rather than including the supportive activities, the table would show an aggregate reduction of 65% in units produced per hour. Virtually all production units in General Technical Services experienced a learning curve production decline of 40% for the first three months after implementing their respective sub-systems. However, if it were only a matter of the learning curve without the introduction of additional responsibilities and duties, the production rate returned to (or exceeded) the "normal" level within six months. The measurement for 1987/88 covers twelve to twenty-four months after the final merging of order/receive functions into the integrated system.

What about costs? Table 4 translates hours to dollars. During the five year period, the labor costs for acquisitions increased 28%.

TABLE 2: PAID LABOR HOURS IN ACQUISITIONS-RELATED ACTIVITIES 1983/84 AND 1987/88.

	1983/84	1987/88	
Verification	9,347	8,119	-13%
Data Entry	3,187	3,106	-3%
Ordering	4,102	4,502	10%
Receiving	6,407	5,932	-7%
Invoice Payment	6,407	569	-91%
	29,450	**22,228**	**-25%**

TABLE 3: UNITS PRODUCED PER HOUR IN ACQUISITIONS-RELATED ACTIVITIES 1983/84 AND 1987/88.

	1983/84	1987/88	
Verification (searches per hr.)	2.45	5.02	105%
Data Entry (records per hr.)	6.34	8.27	30%
Ordering (orders per hr.)	4.76	2.50	-47%
Receiving (volumes per hr.)	6.16	5.05	-18%
	19.71	**20.84**	**6%**
Invoice Payment (invoice lines per hr.)	*	78.68	

*Data not available.

TABLE 4: LABOR COST OF ACQUISITIONS-RELATED ACTIVITIES (PER VOLUME RECEIVED) 1983/84 and 1987/88

	1983/84	1987/88	
VOLUMES RECEIVED	36,071	29,932	-17%
Verification	$2.32	$2.97	28%
Data Entry	0.74	1.05	42%
Ordering	0.95	1.44	52%
Receiving	1.07	1.38	29%
Invoice Payment	0.40	0.19	-52%
	$5.48	**$7.03**	**28%**

Some of the increase in labor cost comes from annual raises in salaries and the corresponding elevation of benefits expenses. To compensate, one can "level" the labor costs per hour for the two years in question. Adding the labor cost per hour in 1983/84 and in 1987/88 for each production unit and dividing by two produces a mean labor cost per hour. If one were to use the same mean labor cost per hour for both years in each of the processing units, the table would show the comparative cost impact. Table 5 presents this data.

It is probable that the impact of the acquisitions module of the integrated online system with accompanying changes in procedure accounted for much of the 8% increase in the comparative labor cost.

NON-LABOR COSTS

Table 6 presents the cost of Supplies and Expenses and of Equipment. For Verification, costs included not only supplies, operating expenses and equipment, but also OCLC transaction costs, OCLC telecommunications costs, and OCLC hardware-based costs. Preorder search and verification relied heavily on the OCLC database. Equipment costs reflect amortization over three years if the cost of the item exceeded $500.

The two most significant changes appear in Data Entry and Receiving. In Data Entry, the inclusion of acquisitions records into the integrated online system permitted elimination of monthly microfiche copies listing outstanding orders. In Receiving, the primary increase appears in postage, a factor not related to the integrated online system. The aggregate shows a 27% increase in non-labor costs during the five year span.

Summary

In summary, Table 7 brings together the costs shown in Tables 1, 4, and 6. The initial cost to acquisition-related functions for implementing the integrated online system was $7,873 assessed to Verification in 1985/86. In mid-1986, General Technical Services activated the acquisitions module of the integrated online system. The

TABLE 5: COMPARATIVE LABOR COST OF ACQUISITIONS-RELATED ACTIVITIES
(PER VOLUME RECEIVED) 1983/84 and 1987/88

	1983/84	1987/88	
VOLUMES RECEIVED	36,071	29,932	-17%
Verification	$2.58	$2.70	5%
Data Entry	.82	.96	17%
Ordering	1.02	1.35	32%
Receiving	1.16	1.29	11%
Invoice Payment	.44	.18	-59%
	$6.02	$6.48	8%

TABLE 6: NON-LABOR COST OF ACQUISITIONS-RELATED ACTIVITIES
(PER VOLUME RECEIVED) 1983/84 and 1987/88

	1983/84	1987/88	
VOLUMES RECEIVED	36,071	29,932	-17%
Verification	$0.16	$0.22	38%
Data Entry	0.16	0.05	-69%
Ordering	0.13	0.16	23%
Receiving	0.02	0.21	950%
Invoice Payment	0.09	0.07	-22%
	$0.56	**$0.71**	**27%**

TABLE 7: COST OF ACQUISITIONS-RELATED ACTIVITIES (PER VOLUME RECEIVED) *
1983/84 and 1987/88

	1983/84	1987/88	
VOLUMES RECEIVED	36,071	29,932	-17%
Verification	$2.48	$3.48	40%
Data Entry	0.90	1.10	22%
Ordering	1.08	1.74	61%
Receiving	1.09	1.73	59%
Invoice Payment	0.49	0.26	-47%
	$6.04	**$8.31**	**38%**

*The analysis omits specific overhead costs which do not relate specifically to the discussion. These are Technical Services administrative overhead, space maintenance, and insurance assessments.

expansion of terminals to the order/receive staff brought corresponding increases in the direct assessment to acquisitions for the support of the system. Moreover, the integration of information into a single system required significant changes in procedures. This had major impact on ordering and receiving. The aggregate results for ordering and receiving showed a 3% increase in staff hours and a decline in units produced per hour of 47% and 18% respectively from 1983/84 to 1987/88.

CONCLUSION

Is the handling of acquisitions via an integrated online system more or less expensive? If one considers the assessment to acquisitions for supporting the system, then certainly there are costs unique to the online environment. On the other hand, one must recognize the potential cost savings which can result from more effective procedures and improved methods of disseminating information.

Bringing acquisition functions into the integrated online system consolidated information and made it more easily accessible to the library staff at-large and, therefore, to the library clientele. This was not done inexpensively nor was it accomplished without long-term impact. If one could assign dollar value to more effective management of outstanding orders (including more effective claiming), more prompt communication of reports between Acquisitions staff and bibliographers and Public Service staff, more up-to-the-minute data on receipt of new titles to library clientele, then perhaps some of the fiscal and operational impact of the integrated system on acquisition functions could be ameliorated.

In the final analysis, the cost impact on acquisitions of implementing an integrated online system is significant. The major impact is on labor. While not all library environments treat the ongoing cost of the system as an assessment to the various library functions, all technical processing units share the impact of increased responsibilities required for an effective integrated system. This in no way diminishes the value of such systems for the library or for the library's clientele. However, library management must not take lightly the additional duties—and additional costs—that such systems can impose on the processing operations.

The question whether an integrated online system will permit more cost-effective acquisition activities is one that cannot be answered in the absolute. The result depends on the management and staff of the library and on their ability—and willingness—to seek and implement changes which permit more effective use of the system. For most of us, the environment is still evolving. Perhaps in another five years, our use of the tools at our command will have become sufficiently sophisticated that we can see evidences of more cost-effective procedures. For the first five years, however, the evidence points primarily at more costly procedures rather than more cost-effective ones.

REFERENCES

1. Doug Phelps, "Verification—Is It Pre-Order or Pre-Cataloging?" *Cataloging & Classification Quarterly*, Vol. 9, No. 1, 1988, pp 5-9 discusses one shift in organization as the pre-order Verification Unit was re-structured into a pre-catalog/pre-order unit and re-assigned from Acquisitions to Monograph Services (i.e., Monograph Cataloging).

2. The term "acquisitions" in the context of this paper denotes those functions directly related to obtaining non-serial materials for the library. When the term is capitalized ("Acquisitions"), it refers specifically to the Acquisitions Unit (i.e., order/receive staff or functions).

3. The Vanderbilt University library uses the NOTIS system.

4. The sum of each person's annual salary plus annual benefits divided by the sum of the number of hours budgeted for those persons.

Costs of Automating Serials Acquisitions

Charles A. Le Guern

SUMMARY. Many libraries which must limit personnel costs and yet add services need to examine how implementing new technology could provide one mechanism to address this dilemma. This report describes the cost considerations of developing a manual ordering program into a completely automated acquisitions and claiming program. The comparison of dial-up access to dedicated line access is described in terms of a reduction in the rate of cost increments. The effect of a growing ordering and claiming program is described in terms of the advantages which computerization holds. Miles Inc. benefited from the opportunity to incorporate new technology into a dynamic library program.

Miles Inc. is a diversified healthcare company with interests primarily in the consumer products, diagnostics, pharmaceutical, and food additives industries. The corporate library, which is the single largest unit of its kind within the company, resides in Elkhart, IN and is charged with serving the information needs of Miles worldwide staff. Our user community consists of scientists, managers, and other principally exempt staff. Many Miles employees are served through satellite libraries which coordinate their programs with our Elkhart facility. The Miles Science and Business Information Services Department is divided into four sections: Administration, Science and Business Library, Scientific and Product Information, and Publications Services. Publications Services is responsible for all monograph and serial purchases as well as cataloging and inter-library loans. We handle all journal ordering. This includes orders for office collections as well as for the Science and Business

---

Charles A. Le Guern is Publications Services Librarian with Miles Inc., Elkhart, IN.

© 1991 by The Haworth Press, Inc. All rights reserved.

Library. Our office collections represent about 80% of our company's holdings. Corporate policy requires individual subscriptions to be processed through our department for record keeping, resource sharing, and maximization of discounts.

In 1981, Miles was using three vendors whose combined invoices represented nearly half of our total number of subscriptions. We began a general evaluation of the entire journal collection including offices and laboratories as well as the library. Additionally, we reviewed and evaluated the scope of our serials management activity and examined ways to promote efficiency.

VENDOR SELECTION

The division of the subscriptions list among the three agencies was arbitrary, for example some were distributed according to addressee or origin of the publication. Although each of these vendors had some share of our total activity, most of our orders had been placed directly with individual publishers. Most of these were single orders and consequently, subscriptions payments were being generated on an individual title basis rather than being consolidated by publisher. Most invoices were sent to our patrons directly by the publishers which resulted in infrequent and inconsistent transmittal to the Publications Services Department. In order to obtain permission to renew any subscription, we needed to poll our subscribers individually at the time their journals renewed (according to our records) unless they sent us the pertinent invoices.

We decided to send bids to all three of the agencies with whom we already had experience. The bids were placed during the summer and we awarded the contract in September. A single agency was selected to manage all of our library and office subscriptions. Our decision was based in part upon their ability to address our subscriptions individually, since the majority of our collection was held in individual offices. We also placed great stock in the potential of any vendor to automate our records, thereby relieving us of reliance on a kardex. In September 1981 all of our subscriptions were successfully placed and designated to begin with January 1982 on a "renew until forbid" basis. Nominally, all of our subscriptions were to run one year at a time, but we expected to minimize renewal correspondence for the majority of our titles.

IMPLEMENTATION

In the fall of 1981 we filled the vacant clerical position whose task was to order and claim journal subscriptions. Although we incorporated our agent into our work flow, this function was maintained manually for an entire year as we developed our collection and marketed our services. In December, 1982 our agent demonstrated an on-line system which permitted access to a database of titles, publishers and prices which we needed in order to verify publications. The service also provided an electronic mailbox which facilitated correspondence for placing orders and claims.

In 1983 we purchased a Lears-Siegler ADM3 terminal and a 300 baud Universal Data Systems modem. The terminal was a refurbished unit which cost less than $400.00. We chose it in part due to its availability. We used it in a dial-up mode and it provided access to our records by title as well as through some additional parameters; shipping address/title combination, recipient's name, department numbers, and subject and publishers' account numbers. However, we did not use all of these access points. We found that subscribers' names and department numbers, in particular, were useful as sorting parameters for our monthly reports from our agent, as well as being very useful on-line search terms.

As our experience with on-line ordering grew, we found we were becoming increasingly reliant upon dial-up to answer questions which otherwise might have been answered through cumbersome searching of our kardex. Also new search modes were available. We could use it to determine subscription rates for new titles. And we could determine easily which titles any Miles employee was receiving.

COST ANALYSIS

We rapidly increased the number of titles which we were processing but our telecommunications costs increased less rapidly. Under the dial-up mode we were billed for on-line charges at the rate of $11.00 per hour. Now we use these services more extensively and our on-line costs have increased from $1991 for dial-up the first year to $5400 currently for our dedicated line (see Figure 1).

As Figure 1 illustrates, there was an increase in on-line costs and an increase in ordering activity. Our ancillary activities, such as title verification and claims, were responsible for the increase in cost but this demonstrated that on-line access was much more than just an acquisitions tool. Our need for a cost justified, yet comprehensive serials acquisitions function not limited to ordering, prompted us to install a dedicated line. In March 1985, we inaugurated dedicated line access to our subscriptions agent. Our initial result was a reduction in telecommunications costs from $400-$600 per month to $350.00 per month. The new figure was composed of $150.00/month rental on the modem and a $200.00 month fee for the telecommunications line.

INCREASED ORDERING

As of 12/31/84, we had 2259 titles on order. Now we have 3611 titles as of 3/7/89 which represents a 60% increase in subscriptions. However, with our dedicated line, our telecommunications costs were held in check. Dial-up communications would have shown cost increases in proportion to our increasing activity, but the maximum amount of time we could spend on-line was the equivalent of one person/year (about 2100 hours).

With a dedicated line, we were able to be on-line longer, but we were able to realize a 15% decrease in actual telecommunications costs from 1984 to 1985. Subsequent increases in dedicated line rates have increased our costs (see Figure 2). It is noteworthy that our on-line costs for 1984 and 1987 are essentially identical, however we added 567 titles during that same time span, which represents a 29% increase in order volume. Another advantage of the dedicated line is that, prior to its use, we never exceeded 1500 hours of connect time, since the projected cost would have been excessive. The change in total on-line costs from 1984 to 1988 has been only a 12% increase. This averages 3%/year which is lower than the increases in the CPI.

FIGURE 1

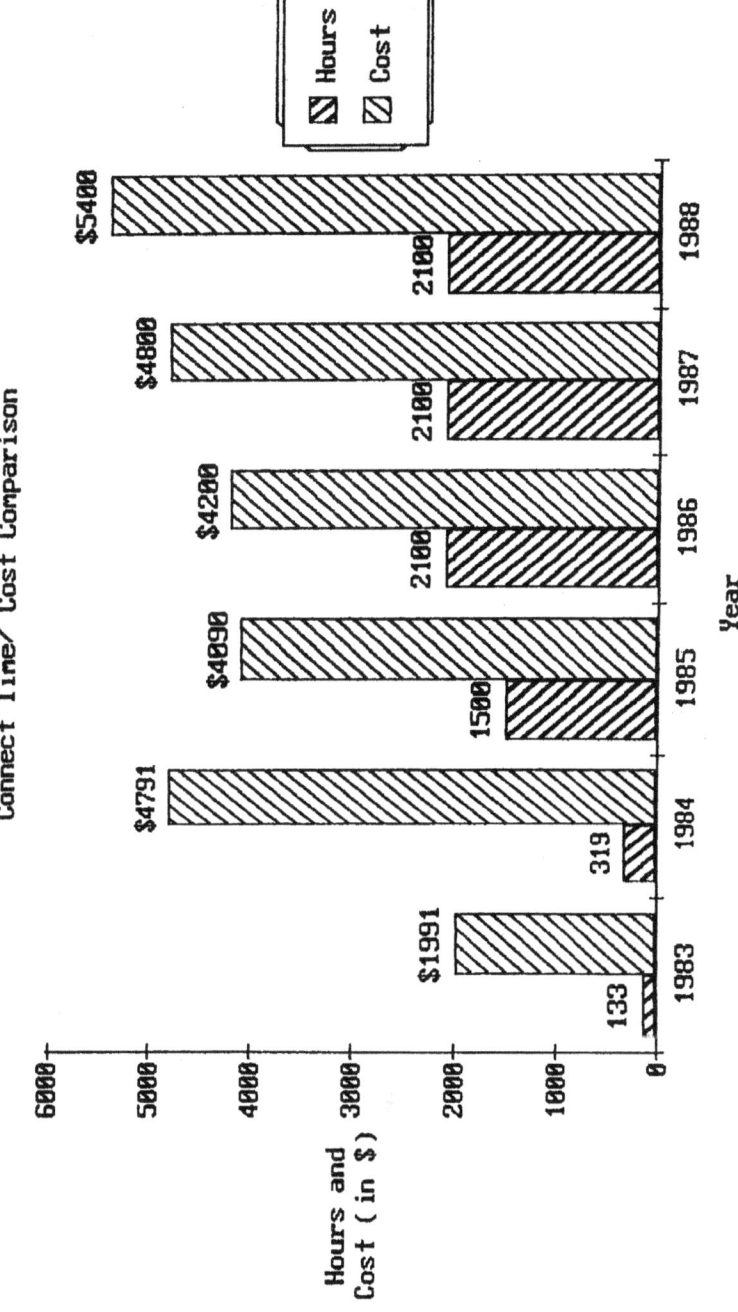

FIGURE 2

Renewals Compared to
Connect Time and Cost

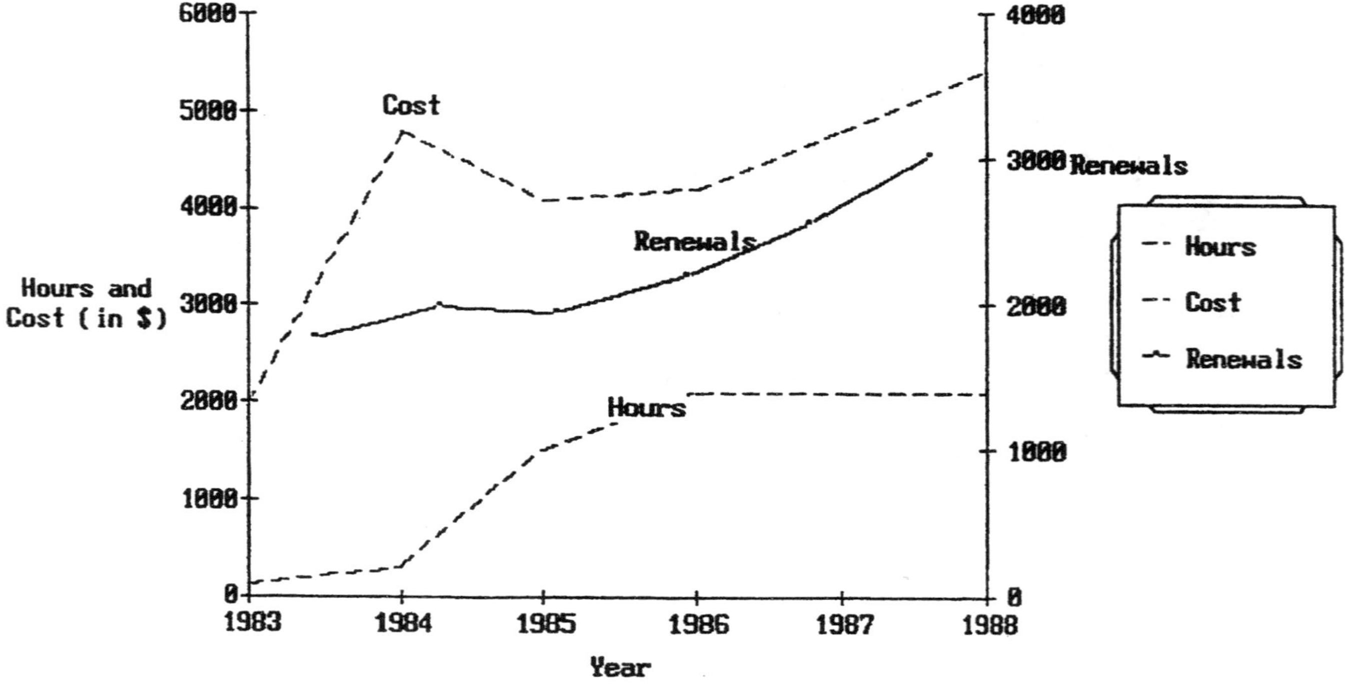

CONCLUSION

Our experience with automating serials control has been favorable. Cost increases have been held to the rate of increase in the costs of the dedicated line and are considerably less than dial-up would have been for a comparable amount of time spent on-line. Additionally, there were productivity gains realized through consolidation of our invoicing through one agency. These added expenses are less than the cost of additional staff who would have been necessary to handle the added volume.

Libraries, generally, are designed to be cost effective in providing services. Automation is one mechanism by which we have been able to increase productivity and provide more services in a cost effective manner. In addition to the cost reductions associated with on-line ordering, we are able to obtain savings through consolidation of invoicing. Rather than issuing a check for each invoice, we are now able to group invoices and issue one check for hundreds of subscriptions. The result has been savings in check issuing costs. For comparisons sake each check drafted represents an overhead cost of $20.00. The total cost for our 3600 subscriptions would be approximately $72,000. Subtracting our agency's service charge our company saves more than $48,000 per year.

Another cost reducing benefit for the future will be downloading invoice data directly via a link to our mainframe. We expect to reduce our costs further by eliminating paper copy invoices as much as possible. More efficient use of staff time and higher productivity are achieved by the automation of serials acquisitions. Therefore, automation presents the only realistic mechanism which permits us to accomplish our mission in view of our rapid collection development.

Identifying Personnel Costs in Library Acquisitions

James R. Coffey

SUMMARY. This article discusses the cost of personnel in library acquisitions departments. The areas considered are: (1) interviewing and hiring; (2) employee attitudes; (3) training; (4) consultation; (5) performance evaluation; (6) non-productive time; (7) mistakes; (8) absenteeism; (9) staff development. Each factor is analysed for cost implications and examined to show how they contribute to rising costs when not carefully controlled. There is an exploratory discussion on measuring services and productivity and suggestions for further investigation.

INTRODUCTION

The purpose of this paper is primarily to focus attention on the factors involved in personnel costs in library acquisitions and secondarily to discuss their impact on the budget of the department or cost center. Ultimately, the goal of this discussion is an understanding of the effective or cost-justifiable use of personnel resources in the acquisitions process.

Having identified and considered the factors involved in personnel, the librarian may carry on the process by investigating the notion of measuring and quantifying them, and then of establishing norms. Whether universal measures and standards can be established is a question for further investigation and is beyond the scope of this essay. However, the makeup of personnel costs can be studied and perhaps be used to point toward ways of managing them

---

James R. Coffey is Technical Services Librarian at Rutgers University, Camden Library, Camden, NJ 08102.

© 1991 by The Haworth Press, Inc. All rights reserved.

which will lead to a maximum result for the investment in personnel resources.

After an introductory discussion on personnel costs, I will consider some of the cost factors, illustrating or giving examples where possible, and end with comments and suggestions for further study. The factors to be considered are: (1) interviewing and hiring; (2) employee attitudes; (3) training; (4) consultation; (5) performance evaluation; (6) non-productive time; (7) mistakes; (8) absenteeism; (9) staff development.

I recognize that, although this discussion may appear clinical in tone, the personal element is not something which is to be ignored in the actual day-to-day functioning of an acquisitions department, and that effective, cost-justifiable use of personnel resources depends on effective personal relationships. If a supervisor is to function well, then he or she has to cultivate first a genuine relationship of personal acceptance and respect for the people with whom he or she is working. While the relationship does not have to be that of a friend, nor does it have to imply a rosy sense of agreement all the time, it does have to be open and tolerant. It does have to give a chance to both people in the supervisor/employee relationship, recognizing that there is a difference between the person who is appreciated and the work which sometimes is not. The supervisor should realize too that confrontation is a positive thing, an opportunity for growth, and that the ability to confront people gracefully but firmly is an essential requirement of good supervision. One doesn't have to take an employee's advice but one does have to be open to it. The most productive working relationship will be one which is at ease and secure whether the atmosphere is quiet or turbulent. Having decided to investigate what is involved in costing out personnel, I am not losing sight of the fact that personnel administration involves the balance of smoothly functioning relationships with the costs involved in guiding those relationships towards productive output. What is germane to this study, however, is the non-personal element and that is what I will concentrate on.

It should be recognized also that there will be still much to say about the matter of acquisitions costs—especially since there is little available in the library literature—and that perhaps ultimately we may find that effective use of personnel is dependent more on intuition than on quantification. Even so, intuition has a rational basis and hopefully, some of what goes into it will be made clear in what follows.

COST OVERVIEW

One of the first steps to take in determining how well money is used within a budgetary unit is to focus attention on the individual jobs being done. Then, having done so, a manager can analyse each task in terms of purpose, rationale, and effectiveness. Next, the manager will consider whether the level of personnel and the amount of time spent is appropriate, and, finally, whether the performance is accurate.

When a task is judged to be well-thought out and performed by a competent employee, then the quality of performance should be high. When there is poor coordination of person to job, money is wasted and the acquisitions department is left open to criticism. This criticism can be based in part on the failure in efficiency and in part on the suspicion that more could be done for less. The acquisitions librarian can be left thus in a vulnerable position, finding him- or herself on the defensive when it comes to allocating resources. It should be borne in mind also that a task could cost too much, that what is spent on doing it costs more than what is lost if it is not done, and that, therefore, the routine might be eliminated.

The first part of the problem, justifying the task, can be easy. If there is a good reason for doing the job, then a procedure can be written and used to process the materials. In acquisitions, the procedures are going to be complex because the acquisition of library materials is tied to making them accessible to a wide spectrum of users. Therefore, the volume of work going into the handling of books in a library is much greater than would be the case for a bookseller.

The second part of the problem, personnel, is unpredictable, the part which can get out of control and raise the cost of the process. More skill and effort is required of the librarian in personnel management than in any other area of the process because there are more variables related to personnel. Anyone can be put into a job and paid; only a good supervisor can get maximum productivity from the staff. The art and the challenge is to hire and train people who can use procedures creatively to get a lot of work done and to maintain order.

Maintaining this balance of procedures and personnel for effective operations is a dynamic effort, one which regulates the cost of the acquisitions department. In actual practice, it is easier for the acquisitions librarian to recognize when those costs have gotten out of hand than to determine statistically what is the minimum budget allocation necessary for effective functioning. It seems reasonable to suppose that there *is* a minimum effective cost and that it could help a great deal if acquisitions librarians could assure themselves that they had reached the right level.

Costs are high and so is the demand for effective library services. Librarians find themselves having to produce maximum service with shrinking resources—and many seem to think that they can and ought to do so. Whether they think so because they can do it and just haven't managed it yet or because some internal prompt urges them on can't be decided here. In any case, producing a high quality product with minimum resources is an interesting challenge for the librarian; but it is not clear whether it can be met. Librarians can go only so far before the personal stress becomes too great. Seldom do we recognize the breaking point at the moment it arrives. Rather than push ourselves because we haven't got time for considering anything else, it might be more appropriate to take an objective look at acquisitions operations and costs and to determine whether we can operate more efficiently. Regardless of previous experience or training, the acquisitions librarian, like any manager elsewhere in the workplace, is obliged to be more cost-conscious now than has been the case previously. A systematic assessment of the acquisitions process, which, it seems to me is called for, could reveal much—anything from confirmation that we are doing the right thing to an understanding of where we can make changes which will bring costs into line with resources. Whatever the result of such an assessment, it can only help the decision making and management processes of library acquisitions to be conscious of what our operations cost and how we are paying for them when they don't run smoothly.

As with other areas of acquisitions costs, for personnel there is not a wide body of factual data which the interested professional can consult. There is some discursive literature; but, in general, it seems as if the opportunities for studying personnel costs in library acquisitions are as yet unexplored. At the moment, there is a growing body of literature on the need for cost consciousness; but not a great deal of factual data available. There are no standards which tell an acquisitions librarian what portion of the time should be spent on what task or how much it should cost. Heretofore, acquisitions librarians have concentrated on getting the job done and not on understanding the costs or justifying them.

The first fact to deal with in regard to personnel costs is that it is the largest single section of the budget. "Approximately 60 % of an academic library's budget is spent on labor."[1] It is probably safe to say a large portion of anyone's budget is spent on labor when both wages and benefits are taken into account. (See chart, Table 1, for hourly compensation costs according to U.S. Bureau of Labor Statistics.)[2] Since this is the area of greatest expenditure, it is potentially the area of greatest savings. The savings can be made either by eliminating positions from the budget or by an increase in productivity; i.e., doing more work with the same number of people. While the first option is sometimes exercised without disadvantage to anyone, the second one is what is more often available to us. What will be examined here, to be viewed as a beginning and hopefully pointing towards further investigation, are the factors involved in personnel costs, how they relate to productivity, and how money is used to pay for them.

INTERVIEWING AND HIRING

The purpose of the interview is to zero in on whether the applicant can do the job well and fit in with the staff. At an interview, everyone is trying to put the best foot forward and to make the best possible impression. Doing the wrong thing at this point can cause the whole cost-saving process to become abortive. The point of the interview is to make it pay for the interviewer. Some light conversation to get a pleasant atmosphere established is called for but the switch to business should take place early on; otherwise the interview becomes an expensive waste of time. If the applicant is inter-

TABLE 1

WHAT IT REALLY COSTS EMPLOYERS

COMPENSATION COMPONENT	ALL PRIVATE INDUSTRY	GOODS INDUSTRIES	SERVICE INDUSTRIES
Legally required*	$1.13	$1.43	1.01
Paid vacation and leave	.93	$1.09	.87
Insurance	.72	$1.02	.60
Pension and savings	.48	.64	.41
Other benefits	.02	.04	.01
Total benefits	$3.28	$4.22	$2.90
Wages, salaries and bonuses	$10.15	$11.65	$9.52
Total Compensation	$13.43	$15.87	$12.42

*Social Security, worker's comp., unemployment insurance, disability, and Medicare

Above are the average hourly employer costs for employee compensation, by major industry groups, according to a 1987 survey by the U.S. Bureau of Labor Statistics. [2]

nal, then the institution is paying both employees to talk outside the context of their daily work; so the talk should be directed to a business-like purpose. It is important to get the applicant to talk about him- or herself and to articulate the interviewee's feelings about the qualities you are looking for. The investment in time and money for the interview is one thing. A more sobering cost consideration is the amount lost in hiring someone unsuited to the job; so it behooves the interviewer to put forth the best effort to making sure that the candidate is interviewed thoroughly. If something goes wrong at this stage, then the librarian escalates the costs incurred later on in having to dismiss the employee and resume the search process.

In acquisitions, the actual hiring process does not usually take long; but it entails analyzing the job, defining the skills needed, reviewing candidates, making the job offer, waiting for an acceptance, and having the person briefed by personnel. During this time the actual work is either not being done, or not done fully, or done by someone else. As long as the hiring process works efficiently, the costs are kept down; but the librarian has to be aware that the productivity of the department slows down for the duration of the job vacancy and will rise slowly once the person is on the job.

EMPLOYEE ATTITUDES

In acquisitions work, in my opinion, two factors determine the productivity of the employee: the attitude towards order and how well trained the individual is. If these two factors are coordinated positively, then the potential for high productivity is there: maximum output comes from minimum input. The manager's ideal then becomes to make the environment conducive to mixing effectively the training process with the employee's orientation towards order. Identifying the potential employee's sense of satisfaction with order becomes the acquisitions librarian's first cost-cutting tool. It becomes personally frustrating as well as financially wasteful to put a person into acquisitions work without the expectation that the employee will get a feeling of self-affirmation from organization and order. There is sometimes another factor which enters into the picture and that is the other people on the staff: while most people manage to get along well and thus contribute to a good work atmosphere, others are difficult and disruptive. The person who alienates co-workers through remote, unfriendly, or rude behavior causes a slowdown in productivity because he or she can be a constant distraction to the more productive staff.

How can an attitude be expressed in terms of cost? It may not be susceptible to measurement; but whether or not it is possible to put a dollar amount on a person's positive attitude, it is clear that a poor attitude, or a lack of interest, or a lack of a sense of fulfillment from a job does affect productivity negatively. It may not be possible to measure quantifiably the cost of one's attitude but it is possible to claim that the library is paying a price for the way an employee feels about the work. While there are other important factors in the mix, factors which should not be ignored, the way the employee relates to order is, I think, one of the most essential. From a study (early 1980's) on job satisfaction among Colorado library workers an interesting fact emerged relating to a high degree of satisfaction with technical services work: "The people who listed these [as enjoyable] activities felt a sense of 'accomplishment' and that they were contributing to the 'order' of the library."[3]

TRAINING

Once the employee has been hired and is ready to start, the process of training becomes the next cost factor to take into account. The problems to deal with at this stage revolve around how good a teacher the supervisor is and the unique way the individual arrives at an understanding of the work. The skill required of the supervisor therefore becomes recognizing the learning pattern and working with it, using it effectively to get the employee to a complete understanding of the job. It is important to realize when an employee has had enough understanding of the job to perform at top capacity. Some people need to know the whole operation in order to do their part well and others need only a limited view. The supervisor has to be flexible in responding to employees and has to know when to stop and when to resume training. The quantity and quality of the output will guide the process and give the signal to the supervisor. More important to the process is the recognition of bad work habits. An employee's tolerance for what is an acceptable margin of error does not often take into account the impact of that error on work down the line. Opportunities for employees to experience the consequences of their errors should be provided when possible.

In considering the cost of training employees, it is important to keep in mind the cost of waste and error from those employees who are not trained well or who are left to train themselves. It is generally recognized that competent training entails a large financial investment for a minimal initial return. The investment in carefully planned and implemented training also is considered to represent a much smaller cost than does the haphazard or unstructured approach. In addition, it results in less waste and a faster rise in productivity. That the time and care taken with structured training will show real long-term savings is demonstrated by an experimental case study at Johns-Manville. One of the purposes of the study was to find out whether structured training is related to cost savings. The authors noted in the study that structured training programs were often dropped for the purpose of saving money. The research showed that: structured training takes significantly less time; competence is reached faster in structured training; there is no significant cost difference between the two methods; production losses are significantly greater under unstructured training; structured trainees can solve a significantly higher percentage of problems; and that there were no significant differences in attitude between the two groups.[4]

If the supervisor is cost-conscious, then he or she recognizes that every activity of an employee has a price tag. Careful guidance to new employees will imply therefore, that the supervisor is paying attention not only to present productivity but also to how well the work is performed at each stage of the process and to what mistakes or bad habits become evident. This is due to the supervisor's realization that such errors can expand exponentially with regard to cost as the error goes through the system. Time spent doing any part of the job incorrectly should be viewed as time spent not working as far as the cost is concerned. The time spent later correcting it is an even more significant cost factor. Anyone who has placed a serial order with the wrong dealer will realize the potential such errors have for taking up time and money. It is evident from this that the standards set by the supervisor also have a cost attached to them—

again, one that is hard to measure when the standards are high and effective but obviously costly when they are not.

How much does training cost? The initial answer to that is that it costs a lot. What needs to be identified are the factors involved and how long it takes to complete the initial training. At first in acquisitions training, the library is paying the employee to learn what the output is and how to produce it. The supervisor is being paid to show the employee how to do the work productively, efficiently, and with a minimum of waste. Unless there is personal resistance or limited mental capacity, an employee can learn an acquisitions routine without much difficulty. If the trainer proceeds slowly at first and does not go on to the next step unless the person fully understands the present one, then the training will take place in a "reasonable" period of time. Taking into account individual learning rates and patterns, it should be clear at some point how well the employee is going to understand what is supposed to be happening. It should be noted too that the library *is* paying for productivity at this stage; even though the employee may not be producing much. The quality of it is important. While the learning situation can be made more relaxed by conversation of a social nature, the supervisor has to realize that this costs money too and should keep things on the productivity track.

CONSULTATION

The term consultation can be used to describe whatever steps the employee needs to take, having been trained in the basics of the job, to clarify the requirements of a task at hand. Put simply, an employee has to ask questions no matter how thorough the training is. Such questions may be for the purpose of understanding the right next step or for understanding the priority a problem should take. The willingness to ask questions is important and the supervisor should encourage it as long as it leads to better, productive work. Questions about work are a normal part of business operations and don't usually entail enough of a cost to concern a manager. What does become costly is the time spent by people who ask the same question over and over, or who ask anything that comes to mind as a receptive listener comes by, or who ask fellow employees when they should be asking the supervisor. Hopefully, the fellow employees are well-trained enough to know the right way to proceed; but they are not in on the training process and don't know how to judge the question in the appropriate context.

What the institution pays for in consultations is the time spent by the employee with the manager, by the employee with other employees, and the time spent on whatever errors result. What is particularly disturbing about the cost of consultation when it is directed to the wrong person is that it has the potential to effect work flow indefinitely and to multiply waste and its attendant expense.

PERFORMANCE EVALUATION

Most of the time performance evaluations should be viewed as an investment well-worth the cost. They keep everyone on track and working harmoniously. While they take away from work productivity and can take a long time in some cases, they can add to the overall productivity of the employee and prevent decreases in output. Costs for this become inordinate however when the personnel evaluation becomes strung out into a series of performance interviews for the purpose of getting an acceptable level of output from someone who has been performing poorly. In such cases the library is paying two or three people to talk about the job while the work is not getting done. In addition, such employees usually turn out a low output to begin with which increases the unit cost at the same time that the responsibility for completing the work may fall to someone else. In some crucial jobs the level of library service deteriorates and causes loss of good will, often an ingredient in budget allocations.

While the cost significance of the performance evaluation in terms of productivity cannot be ignored, librarians don't find it any easier to deal with than any other professional manager. People are not comfortable with what they view as the negative, confrontational aspect of personnel evaluation, whether it be for the yearly appraisal or for the short meeting to discuss a performance problem. The Colorado library study showed that "In the area of supervision, management and/or administration, the clear winner of the least favorite activity was personnel evaluations. Some individuals listed the attitude of the evaluees as being the main problem. But the vast majority of responses revealed that most managers feel very uncomfortable with the activity itself. They questioned the overall results of the process and did not look forward to the time engaged in the performance of the duty."⁵

NON-PRODUCTIVE TIME

A certain portion of the day is spent in non work-related activity and while much of it is legitimate or acceptable, the total amount can be surprising. Every supervisor is aware of times when the staff as a group stops working and focuses attention on something extraneous. While it does pay in good will to allow some of this, a supervisor has to know when to discourage it. In a typical day, with a staff of ten people, it would not be unusual to suppose that 3 people might arrive 5 minutes late for work, and take 5 minutes longer for breaks or lunches; 6 people might be diverted for 15 minutes to hear about someone's new baby or to discuss a union issue; two others are held up at the photocopy machine for 5 minutes; 1 is kept waiting for 5 minutes by a student assistant; 2 more talk for 20 minutes about a serious personal problem; 1 other spends 15 minutes with the supervisor to rearrange the work schedule for the coming week; and 1 person spends 10 minutes on a personal phone call. This is almost four hours of time lost or the equivalent of 1/2 a day off for one person each day. Whether something can or ought to be done about it is another question and outside the scope of the present study; however, there is a point past which this kind of waste becomes too costly for the budget to carry it. Even if 2 1/2 days a week or 130 days a year is an acceptable level of non-productivity, the cost is high. The interesting question is whether this figure is a minimum or a maximum statistic. A prominent personnel agency studied labor absenteeism and the results were summarized in *American Demographics*:

> The average office worker 'steals' 4 hours and 29 minutes a week from the company by arriving late, leaving early, feigning illness, socializing, and making personal phone calls, says ROBERT HALF INTERNATIONAL of New York City.

Manufacturing employees steal only 3 hours and 41 minutes a week.

Executives at 330 companies say that younger workers steal the most time according to Half. Friday is the worst day for stealing, and December is the worst month. Half estimates that the lost time will cost employers $170 billion this year.[6]

However burdensome or annoying it can be to look for savings by cutting such waste, the reality of decreasing resources may force administrators to do so. If it can be done cooperatively rather than confrontationally, it might achieve something. The fact is that lower costs are associated with rising productivity.

Socializing during work hours can account for a good deal of lost time and increased unit costs. A friendly and easygoing work environment can help a productive work force function well. Groups of workers hanging around someone's desk, on the other hand, just to talk can result in a quick and large loss to the library. Some people have a need to talk but they let it divert them from their primary purpose for being there. In an acquisitions environment this need, legitimate though it may be, militates against productivity and is detrimental to an order-oriented, high volume workflow.

Staff meetings, another non-production factor in the work environment, are costly because they stop the entire work force from producing any output for the duration of the meeting. They also can result in lowered output for the rest of the day or for a period beyond the end of the meeting. When calling meetings, the supervisor has to keep this cost in mind. Their frequency should depend on need rather than anything else. Where they are needed the cost should not concern the supervisor. It is a legitimate cost and should lead to better functioning.

MISTAKES

How much does a mistake cost? In acquisitions work, the hole in the dike analogy serves best to illustrate this cost. If caught early enough, the cost is minimal; however, assuming the activity is necessary and an integral part of the functioning of the department, the farther along in the workflow a mistake is discovered, the more costly it is apt to be. From the point of view of personnel costs, a simple mistake such as typing the wrong supplier on a standing order becomes an expensive effort to rectify if caught only when the item comes in to the library. Comparatively, the cost to type a name on the order slip is nothing compared to what the higher paid clerk or bibliographic assistant is paid to get things back on track. The fact that problem solving is part of somebody's job in acquisitions doesn't change the fact that there are more useful things for that person to do than to correct someone else's mistakes.

Poor work habits also contribute to a lack of productivity. A clerical worker who does not batch work when it is possible to do so loses a lot of valuable time; the person who handles every exception as it arises not only loses time but provides poor service; the worker who guesses whether the cataloging copy matches the book in hand instead of asking when not sure also loses money.

ABSENTEEISM

Productivity in a work-intensive environment such as library acquisitions depends on continuity and is related to the work of others. Unpredictable absences can be disruptive to the work flow and can cause a stop in productivity for others as well as the absentee. Sometimes the work of the absentee is essential and has to be done by another employee. It costs money to pay one staff person to do another's job because the productivity decreases since something else doesn't get done and since there is a consequent lag in service. There are employees in every organization who manage to be sick randomly for the allocated number of sick days each year. There are also those who go over all their allotted time and are absent without pay. Whenever this situation arises the organization is involved in expense without any productive result. In normal circumstances, vacations can be arranged for times when the productivity or quality of service is not hindered by absence or are least affected by it. Since the point of personnel management is to reach for maximum productivity from the acquisitions staff, absenteeism costs the department more because others have to be paid or overworked to compensate. The basic outlay for absenteeism, without respect to the cost of reshuffling employees when possible, can be pretty high:

"Most employers spend 2% to 6% of their payroll on short-term disability payments. At major corporations a 1% increase in absenteeism could easily cost the company $1 million in salary alone..."[7]

STAFF DEVELOPMENT

The acquisitions librarian or non-professional supervisor needs periodic opportunities to improve skills or to learn about developments in library services. Conferences and workshops provide this chance to broaden the outlook. Since this presumably increases the quality of the department's output and the efficiency of the operation, it should be regarded as a worthwhile cost to factor into the budget. Perhaps less frequently but equally important, the support staff can benefit from periodic meetings with personnel from other departments or from staff interchanges. Occasionally, the institution's personnel department can offer seminars which are of benefit to the staff. It should be clear however what those benefits are and how they can translate into greater productivity, motivation and job satisfaction. Without those benefits, the money invested can turn out to be wasted. Ideally, the cost of these activities are offset by the productivity savings and increase in the quality of service.

MEASURING SERVICE AND PRODUCTIVITY

If the big question in acquisitions is how to control costs or, if they are under control, how we can do more for less, then the first step is to be conscious of what the costs are. With regard to personnel, a large item in the library budget, I have given consideration in this paper to what the cost factors are and to how money can be lost if the acquisitions librarian is not attentive to good supervision. Each of these factors could be investigated in greater depth. There would be a great value for acquisitions librarians in knowing how personnel practices have an impact on the budget. What remains is to investigate which of two models serves best to guide the librarian in cost control: one would be to measure continually everything possible, keeping statistics over a number of years, and comparing yearly totals; another would be to concentrate on careful training and guidance, assuming that, having inculcated the right training and attitude in the support staff, the costs will take care of themselves.

The first model, keeping statistics, is often viewed as burdensome and difficult to do adequately. If we have to cost-justify acquisitions, then we have to ask whether acquisitions activities can be measured effectively, thereby giving an indication of what the standard should be. We might also ask whether those activities have to be so complex. The need for audit trails and the ability to solve complex problems quickly might indicate that careful, detailed record keeping is justified. It is clear that a high degree of accuracy in acquisitions files makes it easy to head off time-consuming problem solving when the receipt or payment of an item is in question. It also makes easier the public service person's job when an uncataloged book has to be located.

As far as the usefulness of statistics is concerned, acquisitions librarians know when an employee is productive and accurate. It is often apparent, without quantification, that two people will be needed to replace one person or that one person could leave without being replaced. For quantification to have general applicability, the procedures in different libraries have to be the same or similar. So there are problems with articulating what norms there should be among libraries with regard to acquisitions tasks and operations. The factors involved in setting up such norms and then costing them out should be well-defined. The difficulty in gathering library statistics with regard to quality and cost-justifiability has been dealt with in the literature.[8]

Nevertheless, statistics have value to the acquisitions librarian: they give comparisons year to year of how much has been done in each area, they give the librarian a solid basis for discussion with employees whose performance is poor, they give some indication of what and how much one is paying for, and they can serve as guides to reorganization of the workflow. While perhaps not everything can be quantified, the following can be:

- number of search requests searched by language category
- number of requests not placed (duplicates)
- number of orders reviewed by the librarian
- number of orders placed by dealer
- number of monograph orders entered

- number of continuation orders entered
- number of periodical orders entered
- number of orders checked in—by person
- total number of items received
- number of claims sent
- number of cancellations
- number of orders outstanding
- number of letters sent out
- number of invoices approved for payment
- number of invoices not reconciled

If the system is automated, the costs for terminals and maintenance, and for use can be calculated. Sometimes the cost of poor searching can be identified.

Not so easily, but I think equally important, the following personnel factors can be measured:

1. non-productive time: supervisors can take days at random and observe and record the time that people do things that are not work-related. Obviously, there will not be 100% productivity from any staff, but this statistic could give a supervisor a quantifiable guideline with regard to what is acceptable. This is admittedly hard to do but it could give a supervisor an objective basis for dealing with declining productivity. A supervisor would have to be reasonable in using such statistics; but it can't hurt to be aware of them. In fact, they can indicate more about the supervisor than about the use of staff time.
2. interviewing, hiring, and training: these factors, especially the last, can be significant when determining whether a new, and presumably probationary, employee is going to adjust to the department. Any labor mediator can ask reasonably "Longer than what" when told that this employee took longer than others to learn the job or to do the job.
3. mistakes: the amount of time spent to rectify mistakes can be significant in personnel actions. If a ten-second error takes several hours of a supervisor's time to correct, then such simple mistakes add up to significant costs.
4. performance meetings: the amount of time spent and by whom can be a significant cost factor. Just as we keep absence rec-

ords, we can set up a chart to record this kind of meeting by date, how long, and for what reason.
5. problem solving: this is certainly harder to quantify. The problem solver in the acquisitions department can spend all day on straightening something out. But a simple count of daily activities can serve as a measure of departmental efficiency—the fewer problems on a yearly basis, presumably the better the functioning.

The presence of reliable statistics can go a long way to resolving personnel disputes and demonstrating competence and objectivity on the part of the librarian. They can prevent a librarian from making subjective judgments about people. They can show where the effort has been placed each year and they can show at a glance just what is valued in the workflow. While no one set of statistics might be significant by itself, taken as a whole, they might indicate a number of things: whether the supervisor functions well, whether productivity is going up or down and why, what the cost of operating may be, and how employees compare with each other in terms of output. It should be recognized that there is a cost to gathering and analysing statistics too.

The second model, careful training and guidance, assumes that taking care of the pennies will ensure that the dollars will take care of themselves. Training carefully, monitoring performance, and reinforcing constantly will cause the job to be done as efficiently as possible, thus using the library's resources to maximum effect. If the work routines are rationally planned to achieve the desired results, if the expectations are clearly articulated and justified, and if staff are well-trained and at ease with the acquisitions work environment, then the conditions exist for cost optimization. The acquisitions librarian can keep costs under control by keeping the workflow tight and accurate. Keeping productivity statistics by person can help establish norms.

CONCLUSION

Given the activity involved in pre-order searching and order entry as well as checkin and pre-cataloging, the per item cost in library acquisitions is going to be high. If a high degree of accuracy is linked with a high quantity of items processed, then the costs are kept to a minimum. The amount of money spent in the ordering stage may be justified by the need to order exactly what is required as specified by the collection development officer and by the need to be sure that it is not already available in the library system. Once items arrive, it is important to move them through the receipt process quickly and accurately. Since no special time element is involved here, most books can be checked in at a minimum cost. Again, accuracy is the most important cost element. What makes the process go up in price are factors such as inattentiveness to work, wrong books received, missing books, claims, cancellations, filing, stamping slips, recording reports, inquiries, errors in shipping, or loss due to theft, etc.

If the need really is to keep complete and accurate records, then the work requires a given number of personnel who are oriented towards accuracy and high quantity. To some extent, these abilities are with the individual at the time of first employment; but to some extent, they are inculcated by training. The optimum cost depends on these factors. The work in acquisitions expands and contracts according to the time of the year, but the level of staffing has to remain constant and minimal to achieve the correct financial investment during a given fiscal year.

Some areas which could be explored further:

1. the feasibility of keeping detailed statistics and making comparisons among libraries.
2. investigation of the normative ratio of employees to the volume of work.
3. norms for time spent on given tasks.
4. what personality factors are most congenial to the acquisitions work environment.
5. how to conduct an interview for a potential acquisitions employee.

Perhaps others can make more suggestions for further study. If the future holds the prospect of greater demands on the library for justifying its costs, then being fully cognizant of them places the librarian in a good position to continue getting the funding needed. A well-articulated rationale for allocating funds is one of the essential elements in persuading the powers that be to put the money into the library. The literature appears alarmist at times; but it does seem as if, in spending such huge sums of money, we ought to be able to account for where and how and why it's being spent.

REFERENCES

1. Cummings, Martin M. *The Economics of Research Libraries*. Washington, D.C.: Council on Library Resources, 1986. p. 153.
2. "What it Really Costs Employers." *Inc.* 10 Sept. 1988: 121(1).
3. Sherrer, Johannah. "Job Satisfaction among Colorado Library Workers." *Colorado Libraries* 11 Jun. 1985: 20 (1).
4. Cullen, James G. et al. "Training, What's it Worth?" *Training and Development Journal* Aug. 1976: 11-20.
5. Sherrer, Johannah. "Job Satisfaction among Colorado Library Workers." *Colorado Libraries* 11 Jun. 1985: 20 (2-3).
6. "Now Get Back To Work!" *American Demographics* 9 Mar., 1987: 25 (2).
7. "Absent employees hike employers' costs." *Business Insurance* 21 Apr. 6, 1987: 47.
8. Goodall, D.L. "Performance Measurement: a Historical Perspective." *Journal of Librarianship* 20 Apr. 1988: 128-144.

SUGGESTED READING

Bittel, Lester R. *What Every Supervisor Should Know*. 4th ed. New York: McGraw-Hill, 1980.

Jones, Noragh and Peter Jordan. *Staff Management in Library and Information Work*. 2nd ed. Aldershot: Gower, 1982.

Kantor, Paul B. *Objective Performance Measures for Academic and Research Libraries*. Washington, D.C.: Association of Research Libraries, 1984.

Melcher, Daniel with Margaret Saul. *Melcher On Acquisition*. Chicago: American Library Association, 1971.

Russell, N.J. *The Job Satisfaction of Non-professional Library Staff*. Leeds: Leeds Polytechnic. Department of Library and Information Studies, 1986.

DeLoach, M.L. "Human Resource Management in Technical Services." *Illinois Libraries* 69 Feb. 1987: 112-116.

Lynch, Beverly and Verdin, JoAnn. "Job Satisfaction in Libraries: a Replication." *The Library Quarterly*. 57 Apr. 1987: 190-202.

Reid, M.T. and Bengston, B.G. "Report on Technical Services Costs: a Preconference to the 1986 ALA Annual Conference." *Library Acquisitions* 10 (4) 1986: 231-236.

The Cost of Public Relations in Acquisitions

Katina Strauch
Bruce Strauch

SUMMARY. For academic librarians, faculty members make requests for services which are sometimes problematic. This paper states some examples of such cases and gives cost figures associated with the service. The advantage of such public relations, however, is underlined.

"Public relations," Webster's New World Dictionary definition states, is "relations with the general public as through publicity; specifically, those functions of a corporation, organization, etc. concerned with attempting to create favorable public opinion for itself."

Since librarianship is a service profession, we must pay special attention to our public image, particularly in the eyes of our primary user groups. A corollary of the old adage "the customer is always right" in libraries is that we must attempt at all times to help our patrons and to try to make sure that "the right person locates the material that he or she is looking for at the right time."

This series of articles is about the cost of acquisitions. This paper will discuss one user group in academic libraries, the faculty, though all libraries have their "faculty" users and so many of the concepts will be generalizable to them. Defined, the faculty are one of our primary user groups in academic libraries. Of course, the

---

Katina Strauch is Head, Collection Development, College of Charleston Library, Charleston, SC 29424. Bruce Strauch is Associate Professor, Department of Business Administration, The Citadel, Charleston, SC 29409.

© 1991 by The Haworth Press, Inc. All rights reserved.

library must be able to deliver the best possible service to them at all times.

We all know that some library users can be obstreperous, indeed unreasonable. This is the albatross of a service profession. And faculty are no exception. Serving faculty regarding acquisitions problems usually requires going outside of your particular library to another agency, library, group, etc. in order to locate a particular item. Therein lies the problem. We must be diplomats, in countless cases, in order to persuade other parties to do something for our library so that we can "look good" to our own patrons.

Obviously, when a request for acquisition of a particular item is received via a faculty member who comes to see you personally and needs the item "yesterday," this is a non-routine kind of request which cannot be handled in the normal work flow. Just what does this cost? Is the cost worth it? Should acquisitions librarians or collection development officers, or whoever is responsible for book ordering, perform this public relations service? Or should they simply use the time-honored phrase "I'm sorry, but the procedure is ... and you'll have to go through the normal channels"? Is the cost of this kind of individualized service worth it?

Let's look at some specific examples in the next pages and try to draw some conclusions.

CASE 1

A particularly cheery faculty member, Dr. Sunshine, who has been your friend a long time calls you on the telephone and says that he or she needs a particular book by tomorrow. It's five of five and you're getting ready to go home for the day. Begrudgingly, you take down the name of the book that Dr. Sunshine needs and learn that the publisher is on the west coast where it's only five of two. Plenty of time to call them. Taking Dr. Sunshine's home phone (of course he or she wants to be informed of the status of the order once you know), you hang up and go look for the phone number of the publisher. It is a relatively small society publisher.

You call the publisher. By this time, you aren't in a very good mood, but you know you must try not to show that to the publisher's representative as that will get you nowhere. Finally, after explaining that you would like to place a rush phone order if at all possible (and getting switched to three different people), you reach a customer services representative who agrees to take your order.

Guess what? The customer services representative insists that she cannot take a phone order without a credit card number to charge it to. You go around her, trying not to lose your temper, explaining: the faculty member needs this item tomorrow if at all possible; you do not have an account number; you will be glad to give her your credit card number (it's a $60 book) as back up, but you don't want her to really charge the book to your credit card since you know that you will have trouble being reimbursed from your state agency; you are not a member of her organization and neither is your faculty member. You begin to see that it was stupid to try this. You should have told Dr. Sunshine no, that he or she had to go through normal channels because you are going to fail in your quest to get the title and you have already spent all this time . . .

Finally, tired as well, the customer services representative (a nice one, really, who says that this book has been a "hot seller") agrees to send you the book. You reach a small glitch when you tell her that you want the item sent Federal Express overnight so that you will get the book tomorrow and that you want her to add that to the cost of the book. She says that she needs an account number and you tell her, once again, that this is impossible. After going around and around some more, she agrees to send you the book overnight. She promised to get it in the mail this afternoon. You thank her profusely, sorry that you ever considered raising your voice to her. You hang up and call Dr. Sunshine. You have ordered the book and hope that it will be here tomorrow. You will let him know. You go home.

The next day, the book arrives at the end of the day, close to 3 P.M. (this is not a problem with Federal Express, which delivered the book before 10 A.M., but with the fact that the item had to go to the main post office in your city and be sent to your mail room, so it took longer and there was no way to speed them up!). You unpack it yourself and take it to cataloging to be cataloged. When they are through (they rush catalog it quickly), they give the book to you. You call Dr. Sunshine and cannot get him. So you call Mrs. Dr. Sunshine, saying that this very important book has finally arrived.

Mrs. Dr. Sunshine says that Dr. Sunshine has tried to contact you about the book, and that he is not home yet, but will be returning to campus at 7 P.M. tonight. Could you have a student leave the book in Dr. Sunshine's office? It's almost five again and, of course, the student workers are long gone home for the day. You're pretty much by yourself. You bundle up and take the book over to Dr. Sunshine's office yourself. It is a madhouse in Dr. Sunshine's department since they are getting ready for this evening event (for which Dr. Sunshine needs the book) and you suddenly get a glimpse of just why Dr. Sunshine was so frantic to get the book by today. You explain what is going on and ask them to let you into Dr. Sunshine's office long enough to leave the book there. While Dr. Agreeable, the head of the department, locates the pass key, various students are drooling over the book, excited that it is there. With Dr. Agreeable, you place the book in Dr. Sunshine's office. Then you go back to your office, finish a few other things, and go home.

You don't hear from Dr. Sunshine immediately, but a month or so later, he comes by bearing an eclair for you and thanking you profusely.

Cost Analysis of Case 1

1. Initial conversation with Dr. Sunshine—12 minutes @ $.416/minute (includes fringes)—$5.00 (rounded to nearest cent)
2. Station telephone call (10 minutes)—$4.25
3. Professional time to: make telephone call, unpack item, route item to cataloging, take item to department—45 minutes @ $.416/minute—$18.72
4. Federal Express overnight mailing—$12.75
5. Total cost of getting Dr. Sunshine's book: $40.72 (plus the cost of the book which was $60.00)

CASE 2

Professor High and Mighty arrives in your office late one afternoon. He is clearly disgusted and treats you as if you are beneath his contempt. He is working on an important research project and ordered a book several months ago which has yet to arrive. Professor High and Mighty is planning ahead. He needs this book in six weeks. He is getting nervous that it is not going to get there.

As Professor High and Mighty looks on, you locate the order for the book on the library's online computer system and note that, indeed, the book was ordered three months ago. It is a French language book and the library ordered it from a vendor in France. No reports have been received to date about the book, but it was claimed several days ago. You explain this to Professor High and Mighty whose eyes glaze over. He is only interested in when you will get his very important book.

Assuring Professor High and Mighty that you will continue to work on this problem and call him to tell him what is happening, you take down his phone number. After he has left, you proceed to locate an American representative for the French publishing company in the United States and call the number in New York. You reach an answering machine and leave your name and number.

The next day, you hear nothing from Mr. French Connection in New York City. Finally, several days later, you call again and reach a representative with a very thick foreign accent who does not seem to understand English very well. As slowly and deliberately as you can you explain: Professor High and Mighty needs a particular book (you give the isbn, etc., and Mr. French Connection is satisfied that his publishing company indeed publishes this book), you have ordered it from France, it has been three months since your order and Professor High and Mighty must have it in six weeks. Can Mr. French Connection intervene on your library's behalf? Unlike the customer service representative in Case 1, Mr. French Connection is not overly helpful. He explains that the book, indeed, must be shipped from France; he does not have copies of it; no, he does not know where you can obtain a copy of the book in the United States. Finally, he admits that he is going to France in a week and begrudgingly agrees to bring you a copy when he returns. He will ship you a copy in two weeks, when he returns from France.

Somewhat pacified, you hang up and call Professor High and Mighty who, of course, is not there. Several days later, Professor H and M stops by and you tell him what has happened. At the same time, you place an Interlibrary Loan for the book, just in case it doesn't arrive in time, trying to assure that Professor H and M will at least have the book.

You go back to your other duties, making a note on your calendar to check on Professor H and M's book in a few weeks.

The weeks come and go and the library still does not receive Professor H and M's book. Three weeks later, you call Mr. French Connection. He acts as if he has never heard of you or of your problem. You become exasperated, but try not to show it. You repeat all the information once again, and Mr. French Connection explains that you must order the book from France, that is all there is to it. Glad that you placed an Interlibrary Loan for the book, you go to check on the status of that loan and claim the book from France a second time.

At the appointed six-week interval, you phone Professor H and M. He does not seem to need the book anymore. You have the Interlibrary Loan copy, but have not received the copy which the library ordered yet. Professor H and M seems not only disgusted that the library's copy has not arrived yet, but says that his research has been delayed and he really doesn't need the book yet, maybe in a few weeks. You keep the Interlibrary Loan book until it must be returned, but hear nothing more from Professor H and M. About two months later, you receive two copies of Professor H and M's book, about two weeks apart. You add both copies to the library collection, knowing that it will be more trouble than it is worth to try to return one of the copies. You call Professor H and M and leave him a message that his book has finally arrived. When you run into him on campus days later, you tell him in person. He seems uninterested in the book. He has moved on to other things.

Cost Analysis of Case 2

1. Initial conversation with Professor H and M — 35 minutes @ $.416 per minute — $14.56
2. Phone calls to Mr. French Connection — $6.50
3. Conversations with Professor H and M — 15 minutes @ $.416 per minute — $6.24
4. Other professional time — 20 minutes @ $.416 per minute — $8.32

5. Paraprofessional staff time — 10 minutes @ $.16 per minute — $1.60
6. Total cost of getting Dr. H and M's book: $37.22 (plus cost of two copies of the book: $52)

CASE 3

Professor Ms. Grim Efficiency is a semi-friend of yours. You have seen each other socially and like each other, but when she is doing work she is always very busy. On this particular day, you have worked late in order to clear some things off your desk. It is after six o'clock. You have just put on your coat to go to your car. It's time to fix supper and play home-body. But Professor Ms. Grim Efficiency doesn't notice. Always in a hurry, on the trail of a big research grant, she works all the time. Her main objective is to get enough credentials to be able to leave this small undergraduate college and go to a really big institution which has all of the resources which she needs to do her valuable research. She resents mightily that this institution does not have the big resources that the big research institutions have. She has something of a chip on her shoulder because she resents being here.

On this particular day, Professor Ms. Grim Efficiency is upset. She is upset because certain very important books have been published and have not come in on the library's Approval Plan profile. She herself has personally reviewed the profile recently and knows that these books should have come. What on earth is wrong?

Thrusting marked publisher's catalogs at you, she explains each and every one to you — the reason why it should have arrived. You can't help but infer that she believes that you are incompetent and, in addition, that the company which does your approval plan is incompetent because you do not oversee what they are doing properly. She is in a huge hurry doing research, but she wants to leave these items with you and she wants you to tell her as soon as possible why the library did not receive them.

Explaining that she is really very busy, she leaves. Trying to hold onto your temper, you put the catalogs on your cleaned off desk and leave for the day.

The next day, you ask a student worker to check on Professor

Ms. Grim Efficiency's stack of materials. Using data supplied by the Approval Plan vendor, you ask the student to photocopy each profiling record for each item in question. After the student has finished, later in the day, you analyze the copied records against the library's profile to see if you can determine the reason that the library did not receive these materials.

You learn the following: of the fifteen items brought in by Professor Ms. Grim Efficiency, four are already in the library, three are not yet treated on the approval plan so they may be received eventually, two were beyond the pricing limitations of the profile, and the remaining six are not covered by specific subject or non-subject limitations of the profile. Armed with this data, you telephone Professor Ms. Grim Efficiency.

When she has time, several days later, Professor Ms. Grim Efficiency comes into the library and listens to the reasons that her fifteen (now eight) books were not received. Of course, she wants the approval plan profile changed—immediately. You explain to her that this is not possible. A Collection Development Committee, an internal library committee, must evaluate changes to the profile in light of budgetary considerations. You assure Professor Ms. Grim Efficiency that you will take her concerns to this committee when it next meets and arrange to get her a list of items which were treated on approval in her subject areas which the library did not receive because of profile restrictions. She seems somewhat appeased and somewhat daunted by what she has learned about the intricacies of the approval plan.

Several weeks later, the Collection Development Committee meets and makes most of the changes recommended by you and Professor Ms. GE. In addition, you receive the list from the Approval Plan vendor and send it to Professor Ms. GE, who is very appreciative and even orders some of the missing materials.

Cost Analysis of Case 3

1. Initial conversation with Professor Ms. GE—20 minutes @ $.416 per minute—$8.32
2. Student time for locating materials on Approval Plan—45 minutes at $4.00 per hour—$3.00

3. Professional time for analysis of items — 30 minutes @ $.416 per minute — $12.48
4. Collection Development Committee review — 5 professionals for 15 minutes at $.416 per minute — $31.20
5. Long distance conversation with Approval Plan vendor — $7.45
6. Other professional time — 30 minutes @ $.416 per minute — $12.48
7. Total cost of service to Professor Ms. GE: $74.93 (cost of books not included)

CONCLUSION

These cases all are true; only the names have been changed. And, doubtless, all of us have had similar triumphs and horror stories to recount. Few of us are 100% efficient all the time at work; we waste time talking to fellow workers, pursuing avenues that are not profitable, spinning our wheels reading the literature to solve some internal problem.

Public relations is not a waste of time. It is the provider of enormous good will. And it is important to remember this when we become hassled with demands.

Think of this the next time your least favorite faculty member comes by and asks you to do something especially quickly. You won't be sorry. Neither will your institution.

The Cost of Payment: Library Invoice Payment Operations

Marcia L. Anderson

SUMMARY. The objective of the payment operation is to efficiently expend funds for materials received into the library, and in so doing, to create a record of payment and all related financial transactions. This process demands strict internal accounting and administrative controls. Effective implementation of these controls is designed to safeguard library assets, but can also promote operational efficiency and reduce costs. The Acquisitions librarian who understands the application of accounting and administrative controls and utilizes the products of the control systems will be better able to organize payment operations for maximum utilization of resources.

"Paying an invoice may be the easiest aspect of getting a book in the library."[1]

If one assumes that acquisitions "include *all* tasks related to obtaining *all* library materials"[2] and agrees that the basic objective of the acquisitions process is "to purchase for and receive into the library materials requested and/or required,"[3] then the above statement may well be true. However simple, the process of invoice payment is not without costs and, though unavoidable, these costs must be recognized and analyzed by the Acquisitions manager who wishes to maximize the assets and the output of the Acquisitions department.

The cost of the invoice payment operation, like many other acquisitions-related costs is primarily attributable to the cost of staffing, rather than equipment, supplies, space, etc. The invoice pay-

---

Marcia L. Anderson is Head of Acquisitions, Arizona State University Libraries, Tempe AZ 85287-1006.

© 1991 by The Haworth Press, Inc. All rights reserved.

ment operation is a very labor-intensive process—one in which accuracy, production of paper records, and careful monitoring of activities is a necessity. Staffing patterns reflect a library's goal, size, resources, governance, organizational structure, applications of automation, service requirements, etc.[4] However, the objective of the payment operation, i.e., expenditure of the library's materials budget, requires that certain internal control mechanisms also be present in order to protect library assets. The organization and staffing pattern of a payment operation result from the application of two sets of internal controls: accounting controls and administrative controls.

ACCOUNTING CONTROLS

The process (and cost) of paying an invoice cannot be considered by itself. The payment operation is inextricably intertwined with the maintenance of a fund accounting system. It is impossible to sustain a payment operation at any level without some, at least rudimentary, form of accounting controls. Accounting controls are designed to provide reasonable assurance of managerial control and include methods and procedures that deal with the safeguarding of assets and the reliability of financial records. Mechanisms for control include authorization, transaction recording, and segregation of duties.[5]

Authorization limits access to assets and related accounting records or allows only certain transactions to be performed by particular employees. For example, only the Acquisitions librarian and the Head Accounting Clerk may be authorized to adjust budget appropriation, expenditure and encumbrance figures or access and adjust totals on individual funds. Order unit staff is usually authorized to encumber funds as part of the order creation process, while only Accounting unit staff may expend funds. It is assumed that authorization is given to employees by a library manager (the Acquisitions librarian or the Library Director) acting within the scope of his or her position.

The mechanism of transaction recording ensures that the fund accounting system accurately reflects all financial transactions. This process involves analyzing a source document, e.g., a purchase order or invoice line item, to determine the proper account against which to make the encumbrance or expenditure; recording of the transaction; and posting the transaction to the account.[6] The process of transaction recording creates the raw data from which financial statements are prepared. Transaction recording should also create an audit trail so that transactions may be followed from authorization to order a title and initial encumbrance of funds to disencumbering and expenditure of funds. The flow of activities and financial reports "communicate information that is essential in measuring operational efficiency and the accuracy of accounting records."[7]

Segregation of duties ensures that functional responsibility relating to encumbrance and expenditure of funds is divided among employees. It provides a system of checks and balances within the workflow that helps deter improper activities, detect errors, and aids in verification of accounting data.[8] The application of the principle of segregation of duties means that an employee with authorization to expend funds may not also have responsibility for initiation of purchase orders (and, thus, the encumbrance of funds) or for recording of materials receipt information (generally, the activity immediately preceding and allowing the expenditure of funds).

ADMINISTRATIVE CONTROLS

The Acquisitions librarian wishing to organize a payment operation for maximum utilization of resources must also consider another category of internal controls, namely administrative controls. "Administrative controls comprise the plan of organization and all methods and procedures that are concerned mainly with operational efficiency and achievement of the objectives of the organization."[9] The organization of the acquisitions department, the design of all acquisitions-related procedures, the responsibilities of staff, the duties performed by staff, and the organization and retention of records within the department may all be considered administrative controls.

CLASSIFICATION LEVELS AND STAFFING CONSIDERATIONS

The cost of staffing a payment operation is the most obvious and significant cost of paying an invoice. The classification level of Accounting unit staff is usually equated with other functional accounting positions within the parent institution. This can mean that staff may be classified at a fairly high level in comparison to other Acquisitions or library positions. This is especially true in the case of the Head Accounting Clerk. For example, at ASU, the Libraries utilize a Library Clerk series (I, II, III, IV) at University job levels 3 through 9 and a Library Assistant series (I, II, III, IV) at University job levels 6 through 12. The ASU Acquisitions Head Accounting Clerk position is classified as an Accounting Clerk IV (a non-Library job series), equal to a Library Assistant III position (University level 10), while the lower level accounting staff is classed as an Accounting Clerk II (University level 6), equal to the Library Assistant I. This observation is not intended to imply that the classifications of Accounting unit staff are out of line with the level of their responsibilities. An Acquisitions manager, however, must be aware of any concentrations of higher level staff within the department when considering operational efficiency and the costs of departmental functions. This point is especially important if the principle of segregation of duties must be strictly enforced. The flexibility of staffing patterns within the Acquisitions department may be limited because exchange of duties between staff involved in the payment operation and other Acquisitions staff (those who have responsibility for order and receipt of materials) may not be allowed.

In many large academic libraries, the accounting unit is comprised of a Head, or "lead," Accounting Clerk and at least one lower level Accounting Clerk, supplemented by student assistant and/or "part-time" hours. The function of the Head Accounting Clerk is to direct the operations of the unit, supervise the workflow, approve the work of the unit staff, and perform posting and fund maintenance and reporting activities. This employee is sometimes responsible for authorizing actual payment for materials, even though he or she may enter payment information also. The ability to separate functional responsibility for expenditures depends in large part upon the size of the library. When responsibility for functions cannot be separated because of lack of staff, the Acquisitions librarian and/or other managerial staff must take responsibility for careful monitoring of fund activities. Periodic checks should be made to ensure that authorized procedures and policies are being followed.

"Time is money" and this especially true when considering the invoice payment operation. It is essential to the effective management of the library's materials budget that the expenditure of funds be made in a timely manner throughout the year. In order to maintain the workflow of the Accounting unit on a current basis, consistent staffing levels are necessary. Thus, Accounting unit positions are generally inappropriate staff positions to target for salary savings if vacancies occur.

An even more important consideration in relation to maintenance of staffing levels and timely invoice payment operations is the fact that most libraries cannot carry funds from one fiscal year into the next. The consequences of an under-expended budget can be disastrous and costly. Under-expenditure of funds usually results in loss of funds in the current fiscal year and, often, a lower appropriation of funds in the next fiscal year. This situation hampers the ability of the library to maintain appropriate levels of service, meet cataloging production and collection building goals, and has a very negative impact on the morale of library staff and the library's public image.

ORGANIZATION AND INEFFICIENCY

A disorganized or inefficient payment operation can significantly increase acquisitions costs. Late or delinquent payments increase costs for vendors and publishers and ultimately result in higher charges for library materials. The costs of initiating telephone calls, correspondence and statements relating to late payments is substantial. Responding to these collection instruments is very expensive in terms of Acquisitions staff time and effort. Inability to process invoices efficiently may affect the library's ability to take advantage of prepayment or early payment discounts. Uneven payment operations or large number of unpaid invoices hinders collection development efforts and seriously impedes effective monitoring of the library materials budget.

An inefficient or careless approach to payment operations can also be costly in terms of error control. A system in which many errors are made must make provision for staff time spent to correct the errors. The very nature of payment and accounting work necessitates a high rate of accuracy. The internal mechanisms of accounting control are designed to promote accuracy, but they cannot ensure it. Work must be checked and checked again. When errors are made, detection can be slow and correction is often complicated. For example, monies issued to an incorrect supplier will be difficult to retrieve at best and may be irretrievably lost. Often, the Head Accounting Clerk or an Acquisitions manager must become involved in payment problem resolution (a costly investment of staff time). The process may also involve other university departments, correspondence, telephone calls, and, of course, correction of all related records in various internal and accounting files. In addition to errors caused by inefficient practices within the Accounting unit itself, payment operations staff often detect errors made in other units (a direct benefit of segregation of duties) or by the vendor or supplier of materials. These problems must also be resolved and errors corrected. The cost of the invoice payment operations increases in direct proportion to the number of errors made.

TRANSACTION AND RECORD RETENTION COSTS

Consideration of the cost of invoice payment must include the cost of the accounting transactions themselves. Library fund accounting practices typically involve two sets of books: a general fund structure accepted by the parent institution and a detailed internal fund structure which allows for the library subject or selector fund hierarchies or breakdowns. This means that transactions are usually recorded within the library against a subset of the more general budget line of the university fund structure. This increases the need for accuracy and careful checking of transactions and, therefore, consumes additional staff time and effort. In addition to producing a variety of budget reports within the library and monitoring fund transactions in the library budget structure, the payments staff must monitor posting of library transactions and accuracy of library-related financial reports produced by the parent institution. Expenditures made against incorrect budget lines or inaccurate payments to vendors or suppliers are examples of problems which must be swiftly detected and pointed out to university accountants so that corrections are made. Review of and reconciliation with university budget reports is time-consuming, but absolutely necessary for effective fund control and protection of library assets. This responsibility is usually performed by the Head Accounting Clerk, but may also involve the Acquisitions librarian.

The creation and retention of fiscal records can be categorized as both an accounting control and an administrative control. The creation of an audit trail is a necessary by-product of transaction recording and allows tracing and review of all fiscal activities. The audit trail is also important for effective resolution of problems within the Acquisitions department and library and should be sufficiently detailed to allow for concise pinpointing of inaccuracies. In addition, the audit trail is required to assist an auditor, either from the university or some other monitoring body, to measure and evaluate the effectiveness of the library's system of accounting control mechanisms.[10] The organization of these files and information is important, as it is expected to guide someone unfamiliar with the files (the auditor) through the entire range of fiscal actions relating to any particular title. The files will also be consulted by various departmental personnel to answer questions and resolve problems relating to receipt and payment for materials. The Acquisitions department is generally required by university regulation to retain payment information for a given length of time (usually 5 years). Maintenance and retention of fiscal records and files is not usually a significant cost factor in acquisitions operations. However, fiscal records maintained in an online format can be quite expensive. In most libraries, online fiscal information is archived to paper, tape or micro format.

COMMUNICATION

One final consideration related to the cost of the payment process is the cost of communication. Acquisitions does not operate in a vacuum; it is tightly coupled to collection development, cataloging, circulation, reference and other service points within the library.[11]

Payment operations staff regularly receive inquiries from a variety of library departments. Staff time is also devoted to communication within the Acquisitions department. The need for coordination of effort and exchange of information between the Accounting unit and other units within Acquisitions is constant and often has a positive effect on procedural revision. In addition, the payment operation must maintain regular communication with other university departments and divisions, e.g., the Comptroller's Office, Accounts Payable department, Cashier's office, etc., and with a vast array of vendors and suppliers of library materials. Perhaps more than any other unit within the Acquisitions department, the focus of the Accounting unit is turned outward. The cost of communication can be minimized by careful attention to procedures and transactions, reduction of errors and increasing efficiency. However, the payment operation will always, of necessity, require the investment of significant time and effort in the area of communication.

CONTROLLING COSTS

The cost of an invoice payment operation is primarily attributable to staffing needs and the application of accounting and administrative control systems, as described above. For the most part, an accounting control system must conform to externally set standards and is not an appropriate area for cost reduction. However, the products created by the accounting control system can be utilized by an Acquisitions manager to endure that staff efforts yield maximum benefit. In addition, a review of all administrative controls relating to the payment operation should be made. Three areas for review are described below.

PROCEDURAL REVIEW

One of the most effective means for increasing output relative to effort is a thorough procedural review. Begin with the receipt operation so that the handling of invoices from receipt to payment distribution is scrutinized. A study of actions relating to invoice handling may be of value.[12] Review each procedural step with appropriate Acquisitions staff—who performs which action, why, how often, how effectively? What steps could be taken to streamline the procedure, ensure greater accuracy, save time, reduce complexity? Review the files maintained within the department—who accesses the files, how often, how are the files organized, how often are they purged of useless information, how often reviewed for lingering problems in need of resolution, could or does another file serve the same purpose? Review all records kept within the department relating to the payment operation and ask "why" they are kept.

Periodic reviews of the accounting system and unit are necessary since there can be changes in personnel, policies, governance structure, volume of business, or technological changes to the system.[13] Review the entire audit trail. This can be done by an internal or external auditor or by the Acquisitions librarian. Consult with the auditor, the Comptroller's Office and/or the university records officer about record retention requirements. Most libraries retain far more invoice payment information than they need or are legally required to, especially where older financial records are concerned. It is questionable that *all* records relating to purchases made four years ago need to be kept. Usually, copies of the invoice and voucher are enough to satisfy legal requirements for non-current fiscal year records. A periodic review of procedures related to invoice payment and fund accounting is important for maintaining effective accounting controls and safeguarding the assets of the library, but the process can also identify procedural inefficiencies and unnecessary staff actions, thus becoming a useful method for controlling internal costs.

MONITORING THE BUDGET

As discussed above, under-expenditure of library funds usually means a loss of those funds and the future reductions in appropriations. Over-commitment of funds or carrying over large numbers and dollar amounts of unpaid invoices into the next fiscal year has an obvious deleterious effect on the upcoming year's budget. Either of these situations may elicit a thorough review of acquisitions procedures by the university or parent institution in order to determine if sound fiscal management practices were compromised. This can be damaging to the library's public service image and credibility, reduce the library's ability to attract funding, and result in an immediate loss of funds and/or a reprimand from the governing institution.

The system of internal accounting controls discussed above creates a number of financial and budget reports. Internal accounting controls within the parent institution produce another set of reports which relate to the library's financial transactions. These reports can be used as tools to monitor current fiscal activities and adjust collection development and acquisitions efforts as needed throughout the year. Review of the reports can indicate historical patterns of expenditure and encumbrance and assist in projecting future patterns of fiscal activity. Acquisitions librarians who understand and utilize these reports are better able to organize payment and other acquisitions operations in a manner which promotes efficiency and cost savings while assisting the library in making the most effective use of available funding.

VENDORS

Another method of controlling the cost of the invoice payment operation is through the use of a vendor(s). *Vendor* is defined as the wholesaler or middleman through which library materials are purchased.[14] Purchasing materials direct increases the number of invoices the payments staff must handle and creates additional difficulties. Payment policies of publishers vary; invoice formats can be confusing; addresses and telephone numbers change; and the concept of customer service is often primitive. Careful selection of a vendor that fits the library's needs can help reduce operational costs in a number of ways and eliminate many of the complications associated with paying invoices. The invoice format, account statements and payment policies are familiar to staff. Maintenance of library and university records containing addresses, telephone numbers, tax identification information and internal vendor codes is reduced to a minimum. Customer service is a priority. Customized services are often available if needed, but the real advantage of vendor services is facilitation of operational efficiency through simplification and consistency. The result is a significant reduction in payment errors and an enormous savings in staff time.

There are many excellent discussions in the literature concerning choosing a vendor and vendor/library relationships. What follows is intended to relate more specifically to the payments operation. The Acquisitions librarian wishing to choose a suitable vendor, or improve a relationship with one already serving the library, should be prepared to articulate the library's needs. Ask the vendor representative to visit the library. Viewing the acquisitions operations firsthand can often lead to a more useful exchange of information. Ask the vendor representative to present a brief summary of services, policies and procedures relating to payment of invoices to the Accounting unit staff. Allow time for the staff to ask questions and express concerns. Have examples of invoice problems and procedural complications at hand for review and discussion. Review customer service operations—how responsive is the customer service staff; is there one person assigned to the account? How flexible is the invoice format, e.g., number of invoice copies; information provided on the invoice; order of line items; grouping titles by fund, etc.? Do the account representative and the customer service representative communicate and work together to the library's benefit; who takes care of difficult problems relating to invoice payment or complex questions of payment policy? Does the vendor offer special reports (upon request) which compile and analyze payment data? Such reports can provide important management information otherwise unavailable to the Acquisitions manager.

Utilizing a vendor for the purchase of foreign materials offers advantages similar to those detailed above. Establishing a working relationship with a foreign vendor can take time and effort because of language difficulties, reliance on correspondence, etc. Many U.S. vendors now offer foreign acquisitions services and many foreign vendors now have offices and staff in the U.S. Effective vendor relationships can still be built, however, and cost savings realized even without a U.S. presence. Communication is essential and activities must be carefully monitored. Consolidation of orders, greater customer service orientation, staff familiarity with invoices, policies and procedures, i.e., consistency and simplification, will ultimately enhance operational efficiency.

AUTOMATION

It is doubtful that automating the acquisitions process reduces payment operation costs. Many automated systems certainly promote operational efficiency by increasing accuracy, thus, saving staff time. The list of sophisticated fund accounting features designed to ensure accuracy is impressive. Automated systems are also designed to assure accounting control. They regularly produce detailed audit trails, fund transaction data and a variety of budget reports. The implications of this are readily apparent—Accounting unit staff will spend time reviewing data and checking reports that were never produced before. Time savings will be lost to greater control. As Richard Boss points out, "It is extremely difficult to acquire just enough computer capability to speed up work done manually without acquiring capabilities that far exceed the minimal needs. Since many of these 'extra' features are highly desirable, libraries tend to use them. The cost of performing a single task may be reduced, but total operating costs may rise because more work is being done."[15] Acquisitions managers are not complaining. Data and reports produced by a sophisticated fund accounting module are of incalculable value in monitoring the budget and, ultimately, make a significant contribution to realizing the library's goal of efficient and effective management of funds.

CONCLUSION

The objective of the invoice payment operation, i.e., expenditure of the library's materials budget, requires the presence of strict internal control mechanisms. The application of accounting and administrative control systems to the payments operation creates a particular organization and staffing pattern. The effectiveness of these control systems in protecting the library's assets should not be the only goal of their implementation, however. Control mechanisms can and should promote organizational efficiency as well as organizational effectiveness. The Acquisitions librarian can introduce the concept of controlling costs while safeguarding library funds and guaranteeing the reliability of the library's financial records. This can be achieved by developing a thorough understanding of internal control systems, using data and reports generated by accounting control mechanisms to aid in management of operations, and periodically reviewing all elements of both administrative and accounting control systems.

REFERENCES

1. Robert Mastejulia, "Publisher Policies and Their Impact on the Market," *Library Acquisitions: Practice & Theory* 11, no.2 (1987):142.
2. Marion T. Reid, "Acquisitions," in *Library Technical Services*: Operations and Management (Orlando: Academic Press, 1984):89.
3. Mastejulia, "Publisher Policies and Their Impact on the Market," 139.
4. Leslie A. Manning, "Technical Services Administration," in *Library Technical Services: Operations and Management* (Orlando: Academic Press, 1984):31.
5. Robert T. Begg, "Internal Control Systems in the Library Environment," *The Journal of Academic Librarianship* 10, no.6 (1984), 339.
6. G. Stevenson Smith, *Accounting for Librarians & Other Not-for-Profit Managers* (Chicago: American Library Association, 1983)25.
7. Begg, "Internal Control Systems in the Library Environment," 339.
8. *Ibid.*, 340.
9. *Ibid.*, 338.
10. *Ibid.*, 340.
11. J. Michael Bruer, "Management Information Aspects of Automated Acquisitions Systems," *Library Resources and Technical Services* 24, no.4 (Fall 1989), 341.
12. See Steven E. Maffeo, "Invoice Payment by Library Acquisitions: A Controlled Time Study," *Library Acquisitions Practice & Theory* 5, no.2 (1981), 67-71.
13. Begg, "Internal Control Systems in the Library Environment," 340.
14. Reid, "Acquisitions," 92.
15. Richard W. Boss, *Automating Library Acquisitions: Issues and Outlook* (White Plains, N.Y.: Knowledge Industry Publications, 1982)10.

The Cost of Processing Invoices

Marsha S. Clark

SUMMARY. Analyses of the costs of acquiring materials often overlook the cost of processing invoices. Handling an invoice can add $5-10 to the cost of an item. The components of invoice processing are reviewed in the following article. Librarians need to evaluate work flow and acquisitions policies to reduce these expenses.

Of all the hidden costs in the acquisitions department, one of the most overlooked is the cost of processing invoices. These pieces of paper may or may not arrive with the materials, are passed from person to person, are kept and filed so that they may be retrieved to answer questions which may be asked at any time in the future.

Many textbooks and discussions about the acquisitions process give invoices a cursory treatment. They are regarded merely as items to be looked at, paid and filed. Have we stopped to ask how many times these pieces of paper are actually handled before they are filed, and what is the cost of all this labor?

In most institutions, many costs are not borne directly by the department or the library. The final steps in processing invoices, such as cutting checks and storing invoices and cancelled checks take place in an accounting department separate from the library and serving the entire institution.

The costs incurred by the accounting department are charged to the library and other departments together with other overhead costs and charges for services as a single consolidated line on the budget. Since these costs are not visible there is no feedback to the librarian about whether the department is being efficient in processing in-

---

Marsha S. Clark is Head of Acquisitions, Elmer Holmes Bobst Library, New York University, 70 Washington Square South, New York, NY 10012.

© 1991 by The Haworth Press, Inc. All rights reserved.

voices. The acquisitions librarian may remain unaware of ways to reduce these costs.

DETERMINING COSTS

Imagine that it takes a minute to file an invoice. If the clerk who files the invoice makes $14,500 a year, it appears that the person is paid 13 cents per minute and so the cost of filing each invoice is 13 cents.[1] But this assumes that the person works every minute of every hour. If we include coffee breaks, sick days and vacation time, the pay per minute is closer to 17 cents. Finally, if paid benefits such as life insurance, medical and dental plans, and pension plans are added in, the cost of filing that invoice is 22 cents.[2] And this is just one step in the entire process.

There are in fact, many steps in the processing of invoices. These include verifying the invoice when the shipment is received to ascertain that it accurately reflects what is in the package, checking the invoice against the actual orders, adjusting the invoice if materials are to be returned, converting foreign currencies to dollars where necessary, preparing and approving the invoice for payment, filing and storing copies of the invoice in the acquisitions department and in the accounting unit to use later to resolve problems, issuing checks for payment. Related costs include issuing replacements for lost checks, obtaining copies of cancelled checks and check registers when payment is contested by a supplier, and issuing special checks in foreign currencies when required.

VERIFYING THE CORRECTNESS OF THE INVOICE

When a package is received in the acquisitions department, the materials received are checked against the invoice which hopefully arrives with the package. At this point the review is usually a quick one to make sure that everything listed on the invoice has actually arrived. If the invoice has not come with the materials, the materials may be checked against a packing slip. The items received may be put aside until the invoice is received or they may be processed. When the invoice finally arrives, it is necessary to match the invoice with the items. If the invoice arrives in advance of the materials it will be filed and then retrieved when the actual package is received. This adds time and cost to the simple process of checking a shipment.

Whether a manual or automated order system is used, the invoice contains financial data which is usually transferred to the order system or to a fund accounting system. It is also at the point of checking the order file that incorrect items will be discovered. Materials to be returned will be noted on the invoice. Depending on arrangements with the vendor or publisher, it may be possible to adjust the invoice immediately and pay only for the items being retained. A copy of the adjusted invoice must be sent to the vendor clearly indicating the reason for the adjustment. Some libraries return the adjusted copy of the invoice with the books, some with the check sent in payment and some do both to ensure that the credit is recorded by the vendor.

If it becomes necessary to request permission from the supplier to return the item, the cost of the phone call or letter is incurred. Should the vendor or library prefer to have a credit memo issued, the credit memo must be processed for payment, usually through a procedure similar to that for invoices.

PROCESSING FOR PAYMENT

The steps in processing an invoice for payment vary depending on whether the department writes its own checks, whether this is done in the library but in a separate unit, or whether the institution has a centralized accounting department.

If the acquisitions section has the authority to write its own checks, there is usually a person in the department who is a bookkeeper or accounting clerk. This person may or may not be authorized to sign the checks after writing them. This person's salary and the costs of maintaining the checking account and the checks are additional costs of handling the invoices.

In an institution which uses a central Accounts Payable department, the library must prepare the invoices for payment carefully and in a format determined by the outside unit. Usually the vendors used by the parent institution will be assigned vendor codes or numbers. These codes must be looked up in a listing either in print or online and written on a slip called a header or apron which is attached to each invoice.

Various items of information including the invoice number, invoice date, total amount and account number to be debited must be noted on the header or invoice. The invoice is usually stamped with a fund authorization stamp and then signed by the acquisitions librarian or designated person in the department. Some institutions permit the signature to be entered with a rubber stamp, but many require a hand written signature.

In addition to the labor cost of preparing the invoice, the costs of various supplies including the header sheets or aprons and authorization stamps must be considered.

MAINTAINING FILES

The question of whether to keep a paper copy of the invoice in the department or not is an interesting one. Although Ford states that "the maintenance of duplicate invoice files in more than one place in an institution could only be defended by unusual circumstances,"[3] most acquisitions departments do indeed keep a copy of the invoice in their files, even though the invoice is also kept on file in the accounts payable unit. The acquisitions section may want the invoice copy available to answer questions such as how much an item costs if the price was keyed into the book fund accounting system incorrectly, to confirm quickly that an invoice was indeed processed, to look at discounts, etc. The ease of having access to the invoice in the department for checking such matters must be weighed against the cost of maintaining the file.

On the other hand, gaining access to the invoice when it is filed in a central unit may be difficult. The staff may be required to submit a request for a copy of the invoice and the fulfillment of the request may take several days. It is conceivable that if the invoices from the acquisitions department are sent to a central library office for processing, there might be two copies of the invoice stored in the library!

UNRESOLVED PAYMENTS

If a vendor continues to show a paid invoice on a statement indicating that a check has not been received, the acquisitions department may be responsible for taking the first steps in discovering if and when the invoice was received and processed. Eventually, the accounting department will need to provide a copy of the cancelled check and possibly the check register to the supplier in order to resolve the situation. The cancelled check must be identified, then retrieved and copied. The efficiency of this operation is affected by the storage method, that is, whether the actual checks and invoices are stored, microfilmed, or stored in electronic format. They may also be stored offsite adding to the time required to obtain copies.

If it is discovered that the check was never cashed, the payment must be reissued and a "stop" put on the original check. The bank will charge a fee for the stop payment. In addition, of course, there is the cost of cutting a new check. Again, these costs are absorbed by the accounting department but affect the overall consolidated cost charged to the library.

STEP-BY-STEP

What do all these steps add up to? Looking at a one-line invoice as it moves through these processes we can add up all the minutes and dollars.

First, the invoice is checked against the item received. This takes 30 seconds to one minute. If the shipment is correct the material and the invoice go through the receiving process. The invoice then is ready to be processed for payment.

An apron or header is attached to the invoice. The vendor code is checked and written on the header along with the date and invoice number. The fund to be debited is noted and/or the invoice is stamped with an authorization stamp, and the invoice is signed. This process takes about five minutes. It then takes one minute to file a copy of the invoice in the department files.

The invoice is carried to the accounting department along with many other invoices so we might assign thirty seconds of the trip to our one invoice.

In the accounting department the data from the invoice is keyed into the accounts payable system in two minutes, including a quick check to see that the vendor matches the number assigned. The check is cut, stuffed into an envelope, run through a stamping machine and batched for mailing. This adds another two minutes to processing.

The total time expended on this invoice is about twelve minutes. If we are paying our clerk twenty-two cents a minute, the labor cost is $2.64. Postage, the cost of the check, apron, envelope and other supplies may add another forty cents. The cost of acquiring one item has been increased by $3.04 — if there are no problems with the invoice. Again, these costs do not include the overhead costs of the accounting department or the library. Overhead costs may double these invoice costs.

Suppose that the invoice arrives in the department several days before the items. The invoice must be kept somewhere until the item is received and then retrieved and matched with the materials. The material may also have been put aside waiting for the invoice. This inefficient situation can create an extra five or ten minutes of work.

In addition, suppose that the material received is not what was requested or differs in edition, etc. Someone in the department may make a phone call to the supplier to verify the problem with the shipment and to request a correction. This can take five minutes or another $1.10. If the librarian or supervisor makes the call it may cost twice that in labor costs. If the call is a local call it may cost a few cents, or if it is a long distance phone call it may cost almost two dollars. Another $1.50-$4.00 has been added to the cost of the item.

In the case where the library has blanket permission to make adjustments to invoices and to return incorrect material, the invoice may simply be adjusted. This only takes one or two minutes adding about forty cents. The cost of the postage to return the item may be borne by the library or the supplier depending again on the arrangements of the department with the supplier. This can add several dollars to the cost of the item if the library pays the postage.

Imagine a case where the library has a two item invoice with one correct piece and one piece requiring return. If we take the original $3.04 for the handling of the invoice and add in the possible costs of returning the item following a phone call by the librarian, the total costs may be $5.00-$7.00. The library has one piece in hand and the entire processing cost is added to that item. Although these costs are hidden they are significant.

IMPLICATIONS

For the acquisitions librarian to be able to reduce the costs of these processes, some thought must be given to the processes that are actually under the control of the librarian.

One of the most obvious solutions is to consolidate orders on invoices so that many of the steps are performed only once for many items. For example, if the total cost of processing an invoice is $5.00 and the invoice is for one item, the cost to the library of acquiring that single item is increased by $5.00. If the invoice covers twenty items, however, the cost for each item is increased by only twenty-five cents.

Using vendors in lieu of ordering items directly from many different publishers can help to accomplish this cost reduction. Vendors will accumulate items and ship in weekly or semi-weekly batches with one invoice. Vendors can be requested to ship the invoice with the materials eliminating the extra steps of matching shipments and invoices.

Also, for foreign materials it is useful to work with vendors who will invoice in dollars and accept payment in dollars. This can eliminate the tedious conversion of foreign currencies or the cost of issuing a special check in a foreign currency. If the local accounting department is required to issue a check in a foreign currency, the bank service charges and conversion charges are borne by the institution.

Automated acquisitions systems can be linked in some cases to the university's accounting system. Invoice information which is entered in the acquisitions department can be accessed by or transmitted to accounts payable. This data can be used by the accounting unit to build their record eliminating the need for duplicate keying of some information. It may also be acceptable to the accounting department to have the paper copy of the invoice kept in the library.

The institution's accounting system may be accessible by the library through a local area network or direct wiring. This access may permit the acquisitions librarian to obtain information about an invoice immediately, including the date that a check was issued, the check number and whatever other invoices may have been paid on the same check. Such information can aid the librarian in resolving discrepancies with suppliers.

CONCLUSION

It is an accepted fact that librarians need to be aware of the costs of various acquisitions processes from placing the initial order for an item through receiving the item. These include costs such as those involved in the processing of invoices. This may appear to be a cost which is minor but in reality can add significantly to the total cost of acquiring materials.

The acquisitions librarian must look for ways to reduce these costs. Eliminating duplicate invoice files, consolidating orders with a few suppliers instead of many, and working with the institution's accounting department to reduce the paper flow should be considered. In these times of increased constraints on library budgets, librarians cannot ignore these costs.

REFERENCES

1. Salaries vary, of course, depending on geographic location and whether the staff is unionized or not. The *Occupational Outlook Handbook* (1988-89 edition, United States Department of Labor, Bureau of Labor Statistics, *Bulletin* 2300, April 1988, p. 121, 210) lists professional librarians salaries as averaging $35,000 in the federal sector and the median university librarian salary as $29,000. The listing for library technical assistants is $17,792. Using the same proportionate relationship between technicians as exists between librarian salaries, the average technical assistant salary would be $14,500.
2. This article deals with labor costs and the costs of some supplies. The term "fully-loaded costs" describes costs which take into account such items as utilities, equipment, insurance, janitorial services. Discussions about analyzing these costs are found in Constance Butcher, Glen Gessford and Emmet Rixford, "Cost

Accounting for the Library," *Library Resources and Technical Services*, 8 (Fall 1964): 413-431; Betty Jo Mitchell, Norman E. Tanis, and Jack Jaffe, *Cost Analysis of Library Functions: a Total System Approach*, Greenwich, CT: JAI Press, 1978; Stephen A. Roberts, *Cost Management for Library and Information Services*, London: Butterworths, 1985.

3. Stephen Ford, *The Acquisitions of Library Materials*, Chicago: American Library Association, 1973, p. 172.

Costing Acquisitions: An Annotated Bibliography

Theodora T. Haynes

SUMMARY. For an acquisitions librarian interested in doing a cost study of operations, the business and library literature offer much support: background, theory, methodology and examples of applications. This bibliography is designed to get one started. It includes material at different levels, on many methods and approaches, with annotations to help lead one to the most relevant sources regardless of how much experience one has had. These items are only the beginning; many of these authors have been prolific on the topic of costs.

For the acquisitions librarian trying to control costs, there are a number of useful concepts and methods from business that are applicable in libraries: cost accounting, process or unit costing, time and motion studies, work flow analysis, and strategic cost reduction to name a few. These concepts and methods can be applied not only to tighten cost control through work flow adjustments, but also to help the acquisitions manager spot personnel problems, perhaps caused by inefficient or incomplete training or because of employee-job mismatch. They can help highlight hidden costs of procedures, such as imputed opportunity costs of decisions made one way so that an alternative method or course of action is not pursued. They can bring to light procedures that no longer really serve a purpose, such as filing order slips in a card catalog which has not yet been closed, but in which most users no longer look. Users no longer look in the catalog because a parallel computer acquisitions system exists which may not be end-usable but which most interested patrons know they can have searched for the asking.

Theodora T. Haynes is Business Librarian, Rutgers University, Camden Library, 300 North 4th Street, Camden, NJ 08102.

© 1991 by The Haworth Press, Inc. All rights reserved.

These costing methods offer the library manager immediate and short term ways to tighten cost control, or ways of standing way back and taking a larger, longer view for total cost control using methods like strategic cost reduction.

The items in this bibliography were chosen selectively to serve as examples of the type of works in the business literature, or of applications of business methods in libraries. They were chosen from ERIC, *Library Literature*, LISA, ABI/Inform, RLIN and the bibliographies of other works. Because Richard Dougherty has done a thorough job of compiling a bibliography of sources on costs of technical services up through 1969, I have not included sources from before that date.

I started looking for relevant and helpful works in the library literature because I assumed that business methods had already been applied to acquisitions, or at least to technical services. To my surprise there was far more on public services applications, an area to which everyone admitted it should be more difficult to apply the costing methods. So I searched the business literature where the wealth of works on cost effectiveness applications is overwhelming. I finally decided costing methods applied to non-profit businesses were most relevant when you can find them, because profit-oriented business works have so much concern with money making that it is sometimes difficult to see how to apply the methods in a non-profit environment. However, in the end, all types of works have been included here.

The items are arranged in what to me seems a logical order in which to consult them. The general background materials first, next, the theoretical discussions of why one should do cost studies, then methodologies, specific applications in libraries, and finally, bibliographies.

BACKGROUND

Virgo, Julie A. C. "Costing and Pricing Information Services." *Drexel Library Quarterly*. 21.3 (1985): 75-98.

An outstanding introduction to the uses for and application of costing and cost accounting. Initially the author gives examples of uses for costing and pricing library operations and products: support for management decision-making, as an aid to getting budgeting and funding support, setting fees for service. She then explains the concepts and terminology of cost accounting with library examples. Finally she gives warnings about the drawbacks and possible misuses of cost accounting data.

Penniman, David W. "On Their Terms: Preparing Libraries for a Competitive Environment." *The Bottom Line*. 1.3 (1987): 11-15.

Penniman encourages librarians who "have been self-selected and educationally reinforced to emphasize service," to view libraries and their services as businesses and products, that is, in quantitative rather than qualitative terms. He gives a good overview of the business plan needed to change one's thinking and perspective, because to write a business plan one must set goals, determine expected output and be prepared to measure performance against the goals. The article includes an excellent glossary of "Concepts and Measures Common to the Business World."

Smith, G. Stevenson. *Accounting for Librarians and Other Not-for-Profit Managers*. Chicago: American Library Association, 1983.

An excellent introduction to fund accounting for anyone trying to understand or extract information from the books of a NFP organization. A useful preliminary to several of the cost finding methods discussed in other works in this bibliography. Smith clearly covers the foundations of fund accounting, the three major funds: operating, endowment and plant funds; and finally how to do ratio analysis of the financial results and from that analysis, exercise accounting control. Each small section has application exercises with which to practice what one's learned, and the appendix has all the answers. This works very well as a self-teaching tool. The book seems a necessary one even for someone with a business background who is not used to fund accounting and measurement of non-profit objectives.

Stambaugh, David M. "Imputed Opportunity Costs." *Management Accounting*. 54.6 (1974): 39-40.

A clear, concise discussion of the total costs inherent in any decision to pursue a course of action, because any specific project decision not only incurs the direct and indirect costs accountants keep track of, but also incurs imputed opportunity costs, that is, the loss on any alternative projects not pursued with the same resources. An example would be the value of the goodwill of the administration of a library's parent organization that could have been generated by incurring the higher than average unit cost of special ordering a book which an administrator needs immediately.

THEORY

Richardson, Peter R. *Cost Containment: The ultimate advantage.* New York: The Free Press, 1988.

Richardson emphasizes that cost reduction can take place in various ways, implemented with different styles. But, he argues, unless the manager uses a strategic approach that takes into account the need for long-range cost containment, drastic short-term cost cutting can result in increased long-run costs: reduced service levels caused by employee burnout and lower morale. He offers, in a thoughtful, people-oriented style, specific ways to accomplish strategic cost containment.

Figgie, Harry E., Jr. *The Harry Figgie Guide to Cost Reduction and Profit Improvement.* Chicago: Probus, 1988.

Figgie outlines three levels of cost reduction that can be accomplished in a month. The first weekend one analyzes and restructures the organization to conform with rules of thumb on span of control (number of people one supervises). The first week one does ratio analysis comparing the performance of the company over time to determine its best performance potential, and comparing one's company to other similar firms in the industry for performance levels versus cost. The first month one does work sampling of "the frequency and effectiveness of activity at the various work stations . . . to pinpoint specific areas of both worker and/or machine productivity and inefficiency levels." Based on these three studies, for the following year one resets priorities, ranks activities, and hones productivity to achieve peak operating efficiency over time.

Taqui, S.J. *Strategic Cost Reduction: How International Companies Achieve Cost Leadership.* Geneva: Business International, S.A., 1987.

Distinguishes between classic cost-cutting, which "may immediately strengthen a firm's bottom line but weaken its long term competitiveness," and strategic cost reduction, which requires a "painstaking analysis of cost structures and flows" and "a multidisciplinary team effort of a rare intensity . . . but the favorable results so gained are likely to endure." "Key differences between traditional cost-cutting and strategic cost reduction [are] examined . . . and the circumstances where each technique is appropriate [are] discussed."

Cummings, Martin M. *The Economics of Research Libraries.* Washington, D.C.: Council on Library Resources, Inc., 1986.

Cummings provides an overview of university and national research libraries, their history, operation, and future from the standpoint of the cost of running them. Cummings summarizes much of the current literature on all issues related to research libraries, and makes clear why understanding their costs and benefits is important to the decision-makers in these libraries. Several chapters detail costs, benefits, and the studies and methodologies used to determine these, but the broad picture he offers—the total of the factors to be taken into consideration is what's most important here, especially in considering future trends and cost projections.

Kantor, Paul B. "The Relation between Costs and Services at Academic Libraries." *Financing Information Services: Problems, Changing Approaches, and New Opportunities for Academic and Research Libraries.* Ed. Peter Spyers-Duran and Thomas W. Mann, Jr. Westport, CT: Greenwood Press, 1985. 69-78.

A description of the conclusions to be drawn from the Tantalus study of the cost of services in academic libraries based on 1979 HEGIS data. Kantor concludes that library budgets are still tied to collection size not to services provided and warns that as material types change this can be a real danger. He advises that unit cost analysis be done for academic library services and that library management should start to function in a competitive fashion based on comparable unit cost data.

Kantor, Paul B. "Cost and Productivity in Library Operations." *Proceedings of the ASIS Annual Meeting*. 20 (1983): 297-300.

Summary of a two-year econometric study of college and university libraries' costs and operational output: in-house use, circulation and reference service. Conclusions include that "the use of computer-based systems for the acquisition of library materials can produce a significant improvement in total operating costs and therefore in the average unit cost of services."

Richmond, Elizabeth. "Cost finding: Method and Management." *The Bottom Line*. 1.4 (1987): 16-20.

Richmond distinguishes between full cost accounting and unit cost-finding methods. She promotes the merits of cost finding or determining the true cost of a unit of production. She also delineates the problems and issues at stake in applying methods like those detailed in *Cost Finding for Public Libraries*.

METHODOLOGY

Rosenberg, Philip. *Cost Finding for Public Libraries: A Manager's Handbook*. Chicago: American Library Association, 1985.

This has been prepared as a "manual [that] can readily be used by those with no previous experience in [cost finding]." This guide has "an overview of cost concepts and introduces methodologies used in cost finding [and] discusses the rationale for applying cost finding techniques to library expenditures and outputs." It is primarily a workbook for "calculating the full cost of the library activities identified by the library manager." A final chapter "focuses on the uses of cost finding data ... to show how cost finding can be used as a decision-making tool." This book can be used in conjunction with *Output Measures for Public Libraries: A Manual of Standardized Procedures* (ALA, 1987) which helps identify activities to be costed.

Roberts, Stephen A. *Cost Management for Library and Information Services*. London: Butterworths, 1985.

Roberts sees a distinction in the application of cost finding methods in libraries as distinct from other business enterprise management. He details costing methods, their implementation in libraries and includes a long illustrative model. Each chapter includes an extensive bibliography on the topic for further reading. There also is a multi-page glossary of terms.

Vinson, Michael. "Cost Finding: A Step-by-Step Guide." *The Bottom Line*. 2.3 (1988): 15-19.

Vinson gives an excellent detailing of procedures for determining unit cost of production using cost analysis methods. His example is of selection and order processes in an acquisitions department.

Kantor, Paul B. *Objective Performance Measures for Academic and Research Libraries*. Washington, D.C.: Association of Research Libraries, 1984.

Describes in detail, complete with forms, how to collect objective performance measures that could be comparable between libraries. Illustrated by interlibrary loan, the techniques are applicable to acquisitions and other library performance areas. The methods are designed to determine work flow and delay times in procedures and to point out unnecessary procedures or complications for library users. Especially applicable to acquisitions is chapter 6 on "Measurement of Delay by Flow Analysis."

APPLICATIONS

Cost-Effective Technical Services: How to Track, Manage, and Justify Internal Operations. Ed. Gary M. Pitkin. New York: Neal-Schuman, 1989.

This handbook, based on a preconference sponsored by the Resources and Technical Services Division of ALA, presents the basis for tracking, managing, and justifying processes in acquisitions, cataloging and the automation of manual systems. It includes eight actual cost studies from academic, public and special libraries, as well as an annotated bibliography.

Technical Services Cost Studies in ARL Libraries (SPEC Kit 125). Washington, D.C.: Association of Research Libraries, 1986.

A follow-up to a similar survey done in 1982 (SPEC Kit 86), this includes unit pricing studies and process costing studies as well as time and cost data from some ARL institutions. Survey respondents express reservations about the comparability of any technical services cost-study data from one institution to another, and they reiterate the need for clear definitions and descriptions of how published studies have been done.

Hayes, Sherman. "What Does It Really Cost to Run Your Library?" *Journal of Library Administration*. 1.2 (1980): 1-10.

Other authors mention that one should include all costs, even indirect and unbudgeted ones, in full-costing of library operations. Hayes discusses how he calculated full costing for a university library. He describes the services that were provided by the University of North Dakota Library's parent institution and how he derived the library's share of the parent's costs for items such as: utilities, plant services, business services, i.e., mail, copy services, accounting, etc. As a result he found his library's full-cost of operating to be 35-40% greater than its reported budget.

Clark, Philip M. "Accounting as Evaluation, as Reporting: The Uses of Online Accounting Systems." *Drexel Library Quarterly*. 21.3 (1985): 61-74.

Clark discusses the uses of accounting, how accounts are structured, the usefulness of the account data recorded. Especially if the account data is detailed and the accounting system computerized (even on a micro), this data can be used to guide management decision making using "what if" changes in a scenario that can be modeled with a spreadsheet program. For example, "what if" several branch libraries had shorter hours and the freed staff traveled to provide more staff in the main library; what would be the effect on the overall library system budget and services?

Leung, Shirley W. "Study of the Cataloging Costs at the University of California, Riverside." *Technical Services Quarterly*. 5.1 (1987): 57-66.

A cost finding method for variable costing of three levels of cataloging at UC Riverside. A simple method with forms and procedures that is usable in other libraries and probably for other library functions besides cataloging.

BIBLIOGRAPHIES

Dougherty, Richard M. and Leonard, Lawrence E. *Management and Costs of Technical Processes: A Bibliographical Review, 1876-1969*. Metuchen, NJ: The Scarecrow Press, Inc., 1970.

A fairly comprehensive bibliography of sources on cost studies of library technical services functions. No annotations, but the articles which the authors consider most outstanding are starred. The items are grouped by the function they cover or the method they describe.

Aren, Lisa J. and Webreck, Susan J. with contributions from Mark Patrick. "Costing Library Operations – A Bibliography." *Collection Building*. 8.3 (1986): 23-28.

Primarily concerned with measuring costs of public service functions, this annotated bibliography does have some items related to technical services, and most useful, it includes classic methodology works from business and library literature.

Hayes, Sherman. "Costs, Costs, Costs . . . Give Me a Break: a Brief Bibliography." *The Bottom Line*. 2.3 (1988): 30-33.

A gathering together of recent articles and books on costs of all functions in all types of libraries, with short comments on some items.

For Product Safety Concerns and Information please contact our EU representative GPSR@taylorandfrancis.com
Taylor & Francis Verlag GmbH, Kaufingerstraße 24, 80331 München, Germany

www.ingramcontent.com/pod-product-compliance
Lightning Source LLC
Chambersburg PA
CBHW052133300426
44116CB00010B/1877